SCHOFIELD'S

To those people who have taught us,
inspired us, helped us and given us a
chance. To you this book is dedicated.
We are indebted.

Here's to You!

An Hachette UK Company

www.hachette.co.uk

First published in Great Britain in 2019 by
Kyle Books, an imprint of Kyle Cathie Ltd

Carmelite House
50 Victoria Embankment
London EC4Y 0DZ
www.kylebooks.co.uk

ISBN: 978 0 85783 7325

Text copyright 2019 © Joe and Daniel Schofield

Design and layout copyright 2019 © Kyle Cathie Ltd

Distributed in the US by Hachette Book Group, 1290 Avenue
of the Americas, 4th and 5th Floors, New York, NY 10104

Distributed in Canada by Canadian Manda Group, 664
Annette St., Toronto, Ontario, Canada M6S 2C8

Joe and Daniel Schofield are hereby identified as the
authors of this work in accordance with Section 77 of the
Copyright, Designs and Patents Act 1988.

Publisher: Jo Copestick
Editor: Hannah Coughlin
Design: Evi-O.Studio | Evi O. & Susan Le
Photography: Ed Schofield
Drink styling: Liam Cotter & Matthew Robertson
for Heads, Hearts & Tails
Production: Lisa Pinnell

A Cataloguing in Publication record for this title is available
from the British Library

Printed and bound in China

10 9 8 7 6 5 4 3 2 1

All recipes serve one.

JOE & DANIEL SCHOFIELD

SCHOFIELD'S
FINE AND CLASSIC
COCKTAILS

PHOTOGRAPHY BY ED SCHOFIELD

KYLE BOOKS

CONTENTS

Born and raised on the outskirts of Manchester, Joe and Daniel Schofield started working in hospitality when they were in their early teenage years.

Bartending was not the obvious career path as, for the last 120 years, the Schofield family business had been in fire protection equipment. However, it's now the new family trade as both brothers are now recognized internationally as two of the world's best bartenders. Joe is the first bartender to win International Bartender of the Year at the Tales of the Cocktail Spirited Awards and Bartender's Bartender at The World's 50 Best Bars. And Daniel was also nominated as Bartender of the Year by the Class Bar Awards.

As of 2019, the brothers have spent, collectively, over 25 years working in some of the world's best bars across the globe. From Singapore, Paris, Sydney and, of course, their hometown of Manchester, to the mecca of any discerning cocktail mixer, The American Bar at The Savoy Hotel, London, they have had the privilege of working with some incredibly talented people, many of whom have generously contributed to this book.

INTRODUCTION

Why did we want to write a book? Well, first and foremost, we wanted to share our recipes and our way of doing things. There are thousands of cocktails you can make and so many different recipes for them and techniques you can use that it can seem intimidating when you're simply at home and want to mix a great drink. However, we have spent a lot of time throughout our careers constantly adjusting and improving, so this collection of recipes is, in our humble opinion, the way we personally think they taste best. Our intention is to be transparent, to share our thought processes, and, whether you're a home enthusiast or a young barkeep, to help create truly great drinks.

We love the history of cocktails, where they come from and who invented them, and why and how, and so we've tried to provide a little background in the introduction to each recipe. We also understand the importance of looking to the past before looking to the future and so, when putting together our compilation of 100 Classic Cocktails, we have studied all the old great cocktail books to see how they have evolved through time. This is what makes a drink a classic, as over the years it has been subtly tweaked and adjusted here and there to keep up with modern preferences and habits, so it never falls out of fashion.

Tastes change perpetually and, as bartenders, it is our duty to adapt and evolve with these changes. This book is therefore our collection of classics, which means our personal favourites and also the favourites of everyone at every bar, no matter where they are in the world. We've tweaked them slightly, added our own spin to keep up with the times and to give you a recipe that you can make behind a bar or at home.

Some of these recipes are fairly recent inventions – the Breakfast Martini, the Penicillin or the Tommy's Margarita, for example – which all became almost instant classics the moment they were conceived, and we're very fortunate that their creators, Salvatore Calabrese, Sam Ross and Julio Bermejo, have very generously contributed their personal recipes to this book.

Anyway, we hope you like our selection and hope it inspires you to start tweaking and adjusting to suit your own tastes and preferences, and love of cocktail mixing and experimenting – that's why it is such great fun!

So, let's start with the basics....

GUEST RECIPES

We are fortunate in our career to have met some incredibly talented people along the way. They are people who inspire us to be better, and many of them we are proud to call dear friends. These friends are some of the world's best bartenders and we are very grateful to them for sharing their own recipes in this book. Most are in a relatively classic style, meaning that you don't need expensive laboratory equipment to make them - they're just honest, simple and delicious drinks. These recipes have been unchanged from the way they were provided, spirits et al. We just converted from oz to ml for a more consistent approach.

You will also find the drinks that we consider our signatures, for Joe it is the William Wallace (page 65) and for Daniel it is the Padrino (page 117).

BEVERAGE PHILOSOPHIES

We would like to begin by sharing our ideas on the way we think drinks should be served and created. Here are our core beliefs:

1

FLAVOUR COMES FIRST. We cannot emphasize this enough. What is the point of using hi-tech apparatus, beautiful glass-ware and innovative garnishes if the actual drink in the glass is not up to scratch? Of course, the extras can help enhance the flavour and the experience in general, but really, a great cocktail should taste as fantastic in delicate Japanese stemware as it would in a regular glass you'd find in your local dive bar.

And following on from this, the ingredients of a cocktail should only be selected on the basis of flavour, nothing more, nothing less. Sourcing obscure ingredients from the other side of the world can be fun and can also be a great way of sparking curiosity and intrigue on a cocktail menu. However, it should never come before taste.

And finally, always taste your drinks. This is the only way to improve your palate and make sure that the drink is perfect before it is served to your dear guests.

2

AFTER FLAVOUR COMES AROMA. Research studies have found that over 80 per cent of flavour comes from a process called "retronasal olfaction". This is when aroma or odour molecules travel from the oral cavity into the nose while we are eating and drinking, and explains why a lemon twist or a sprig of mint is often the definitive finishing touch on drinks that have now been classics for over a century.

3

CONSIDER THE OTHER SENSES TOO. Think visually. Chefs are always very keen to tell you that "you eat with your eyes first" and there's so much truth to this. We firmly believe that a drink should look appealing to the person you serve it to as it can enhance the flavour. And it's not always about the cherry on top and crazy garnishes, as sometimes simplicity is key. But remember, presenta-tion should definitely be considered and every drink should look inviting and easy on the eye.

4

GARNISHES can play a pivotal role in a cocktail (see page 9) but they really need to earn their place, aesthetically or aromatically. They should always add something to the drink, and never be a distraction from the overall flavour. On our training programme at SCHOFIELD'S, we emphasize the importance and beauty of simplicity as we believe this is such a key component in any drink that's stood the test of time. In our time behind the bar, we have experimented quite heavily with garnishes, almost to the point where they began to resemble a creation by a pastry chef. And yet, the liquid in the glass was still the most important thing.

5

HAPTIC PERCEPTION. Have you heard about "haptic perception"? This is also something to consider. It means "the ability to grasp something", so the look and touch and feel of a thing, which are integral to the experience of it. So if an Old Fashioned is served in a heavy decorative rocks glass, the drink feels rich and luxurious. However, if a Negroni was served in the same vessel, the heaviness of the glass might mean that you would lose some of the floral and aromatic top notes, which are highlighted if served in a thin, light, elegant glass.

6

COCKTAILS ARE ALL ABOUT EXPERIMENTATION – it's what makes it such fun. And when we do it, we always take inspiration from classic drinks, as these are such a great reference point. Drinks are all about creating a balance, offsetting the sweetness in a liqueur with a dry spirit or sour citrus, for example, and in classic drinks a winning formula is already there. Take a classic Daisy – a simple combination of a spirit, a liqueur, citrus and a touch of sugar. Each one of those ingredients can be substituted for something else. For example, you can swap the base spirit, the liqueur or the citrus to create new drinks. Perhaps the measurements may have to change slightly but the DNA of the classic drink is still there. Almost every single drink we have created can be referenced back to a classic cocktail in this way and, in our experience of working in restaurants, we've found that chefs often work in the same fashion. There is almost always a classic touchstone. Experimentation is where you suddenly stumble across something great, so have a go.

7

CONCEPT is also very important, especially in the drinks industry as, if you're serving a Tiki drink in a dive bar, something doesn't feel quite right, and inevitably the venue doesn't stay open too long. You have to match the concept to the venue and, similarly, if you're throwing a party at home or in a venue, everything has to match up conceptually. Champagne is, of course, what you would serve to guests at a wedding, rather than, say, a Zombie, and a cleverly designed cocktail for a special occasion can really help it go with a swing.

8

"KAIZEN" is a glorious term from Japan, which essentially translates as "continuous improvement". It is normally applied to the world of business, but we love it as a mindset that is relevant to everything you do. The best drinks are made when you are 100 per cent focused on the task at hand. We should always be looking for ways to improve and evolve as it's only through devotion and dedication that we can get closer to perfection. We also believe that you should always try your best at making any drink, whether that is a flat white coffee or a Coca-Cola with ice and lemon, it should still be to the best of your ability.

9

KNOWLEDGE IS SO IMPORTANT – especially for barkeeps. Know your drinks, of all kinds: cocktails, spirits, wine, beer, soft drinks, coffee, etc. In the UK, wine accounts for roughly 35 per cent of alcoholic beverage sales and yet so many bartenders know very little about it and instead, know a lot about an obscure cocktail from the 1920s, which they might make only a handful of times. This doesn't make sense. It was something that Declan McGurk drilled into to us when Joe was working at The Savoy, and it has stayed with us ever since.

10

HOSPITALITY. This should almost be at the very top of our list of core beliefs as, in our view, it's the most important part of the experience. Without great hospitality you cannot have a great drink. We often look back at some of the best bar experiences we've had and, in a small handful of those scenarios, a great cocktail was made, but in each and every one, a great bartender was present. Having a warm, caring and welcoming host can turn the worst of days into one of the most memorable, and that is what a great drink is all about.

Obviously, when you work a bar, there are challenging times, and we've learned over the years to try to avoid making bespoke cocktails for guests. There is a world of great classic cocktails to choose from and so really it is unnecessary. Additionally, there is nothing more disappointing for a guest than to return to a bar and find that their favourite bespoke cocktail is unavailable because the bartender who created it is not working that night. However, we also try never to disappoint and it can be a difficult balance to try to achieve both! But who said hospitality was black and white? There is always a grey area, and we believe that hospitality is always at its best when it comes from the heart and someone believing what they are doing is right.

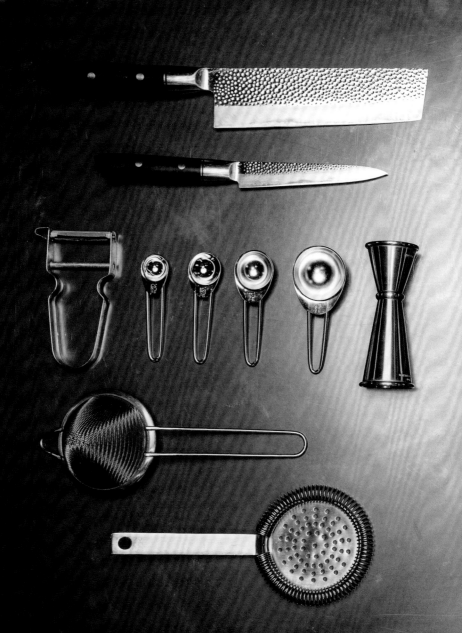

BARWARE

Here's a comprehensive list of equipment that no self-respecting cocktail lover should be without. The list below explains each piece of equipment pictured on pages 12–13, from top to bottom, left to right.

KNIVES

A bartender should invest in good knives in the same way that a chef would. We see way too many cheap knives being bought and thrown away on a regular basis. Why not take pride in your equipment? Learn how to sharpen them – it's a great skill to have in life and you are far more likely to injure yourself on a blunt knife than a sharp one. When using knives, always point them away from your body and keep your fingers out of the way!

CITRUS PEELER

A good peeler will save you a lot of time. We like the steel Y-style versions as they take off just the right amount of peel, without the pith that can add unwanted bitterness to a drink.

CHEF SPOONS

These are used in the same way as a jigger, to measure small quantities. Most recipes in this book use a combination of the two. We highly recommend them for measuring, roughly about 2 dashes is 1.25ml and 4 dashes is about 2.5ml of bitters.

JIGGER

A jigger is essentially a measuring tool for drinks and, without one, you will never achieve consistently accurate and balanced cocktails. Some people prefer to work without jiggers, in a style called "free-pouring". Of course it's a lot faster to make drinks this way, but it can yield inconsistent results. A cocktail recipe is a very precise thing and it is very important to follow it as closely as you can. We say, always fill to the line of the measure. Jiggers come in a wide range of sizes and styles, but we recommend you find one that has been government-stamped, as these are legally checked for accuracy. We have measured our recipes in this book in millilitres as we feel this unit of measure is the best for accuracy. However, we have also provided the equivalent in fluid ounces.

FINE STRAINER

This is a metal strainer with extra-fine mesh and, for every drink that we shake, we like to use one of these. It strains out even the smallest shards of ice and so results in the drink having a beautifully silky texture. Other people are not so keen as they believe a fine strainer can remove the air bubbles in a drink, which can be true to some extent. However, if shaken long and hard enough, there should still be a nice fine layer of bubbles on top and, without the ice chips, there is also no risk of dilution.

STRAINER

This is a type of metal sieve that fits over the top of a mixing glass/tin or two-piece shaker and allows only the liquid through as you pour the drink. There are two common types, the Hawthorne and the Julep. The former is shaped like a disc and the latter is shaped like a bowl.

BAR SPOON

This is a long-handled spoon that is long enough to reach the bottom of a mixing tin or glass. They hold about 5ml of liquid (roughly the same as a teaspoon) and, in an ideal world, should only ever be used for stirring, churning or mixing.

THREE-PIECE SHAKER

These are also called Standard or Cobbler Shakers. They are like the two-piece, but they come with a built-in strainer and so they're a little more complicated to use in terms of shaking. However, as the drink is strained as you pour, they are much easier to use for the non-professional and are very efficient for making cocktails.

MIXING TIN

This is for stirring to mix a drink with ice, rather than shaking it. You can also get mixing glasses, but we prefer to use a tin as the stainless steel helps chill the cocktail at a faster rate and, like

their shaker counterparts, they're much more durable. A good mixing glass or tin should have a little lip for pouring your drink after you have diluted and chilled it to perfection.

MUDDLER

This is shaped like a pestle and performs the same job – it mashes or "muddles" to break down and release the oils and juices and flavours of certain ingredients. Traditionally, muddlers were wooden, but now they are commonly made out of plastic. We generally use one for muddling fresh fruit, or crushing citrus peel into caster sugar. More on this later.

TWO-PIECE SHAKER

Also known as a Boston or French Shaker, a two-piece shaker is a fine, uncomplicated tool, consisting of two tins that allow for the drink to be shaken. In our opinion, they should be metal rather than glass as this makes them lighter, more durable and less prone to shatter. Also, stainless steel can reach low temperatures extremely quickly and retain them, which is exactly what you're after.

CHOPPING BOARD

Have one that you preserve just for making drinks, and keep it nice and clean. This is good food hygiene practice but can also prevent unwanted flavours transferring from your board to your ingredients. When you use it, place it over a towel to ensure it doesn't slip.

GLASSWARE

To create a great cocktail, you need to chill your glassware. Putting it into the freezer approximately 30 minutes before serving should suffice. There are, of course, a couple of exceptions, as Champagne flutes and wine glasses should never be stored there. Sparkling wine loses carbonation when it comes into contact with frozen glass and it can also cause the wine to "close", meaning it can lose its delicate aromas and flavours.

However, in general, cocktail glasses should be chilled as they help the drink to stay cold for longer. If you have limited space, prioritize glasses that are served without ice, such as your coupettes and martini glasses. If you don't have access to a freezer, the best alternative is to fill the glass with crushed ice and swirl it around a few times to bring down the temperature.

HOT GLASSWARE

Following the same logic as above, it is always worth bringing up the temperature of glass that is used for a hot drink, for example a Hot Toddy, as it helps you retain the desired temperature for longer. This can be achieved very simply by rinsing the glass with hot water. Some people also like to use this technique when making an Irish Coffee. However, we don't in this instance as we like to keep the contrast between the hot coffee and cold vanilla cream for as long as possible.

HANDLING GLASSWARE

When handling glassware, always remember to hold the bottom of the glass or the stem. This not only keeps fingerprints off the frozen glass as well as maintaining hygiene protocols, but also prevents any heat transfer from your hands to the glass if using stemware.

Don't forget that it is also very important to check the glass for quality and to ensure it has been correctly polished, with no dirty marks or cracks. Check the rim for chips too as these can result in a build-up of bacteria, and chipped glasses should be disposed of safely.

1. Champagne Flute

2. Martini Glass

3. Coupette

4. Rocks Glass

5. Highball

6. Fizz Glass

7. Julep Tin

8. Irish Coffee
9. Toddy
10. Hurricane

ICE

For us, the most important ingredient in a cocktail is the ice. Does that sound strange? However, without great-quality ice you can't have a great-quality cocktail, as it controls the temperature of the drink and the extent of its dilution. Many drinks are both shaken or stirred with ice, and then also served over ice, which means that dilution can occur during both these stages. You want your ice to chill your drink but not to over-dilute the flavours.

We recommend using block ice (see below), but if this is impossible, then use the best-quality ice you can source. Storing ice inside glassware in the freezer saves space as well as time during prep. Take it out of the freezer after you have shaken or stirred your drink but while it is still inside the shaker or tin. If prepared correctly, the temperature of your drink should be below 0°C and, if you move quickly, you will not risk your drink becoming diluted.

CUBED ICE

Large cubes of ice are ideal for shaking, and brands such as Hoshizaki or Kold Draft produce excellent ice for this purpose, with cubes that are around 2.5cm (1in) square.

CRUSHED ICE

This should only ever be used for drinks like Mojitos or Swizzles, or it can help add some much-needed dilution to potent drinks, such as a Zombie. Some drinks also call for a crushed ice "cap" added to the top of the drink to help keep the garnish stable. Hence why the mint sprigs always stand to attention at the top of a Mojito. The rule of thumb is, the larger the shards, the better.

BLOCK ICE

The density and clarity of block ice create a delicious and beautiful-looking drink, while keeping the flavours sharp for longer. These days, it is possible to buy it pre-cut, which makes it very easy to work with as it's shaped symmetrically to fit in a glass, or in huge blocks, which you must cut down. There are some great moulds available too!

However, if you find it impossible to source, there are some great ways to make it at home. Our friend, Camper English, developed a great method. All you need is an insulated container, such as a Thermos, as when you fill this with water (without a lid and leaving a little room for expansion), the insulation slows down the freezing process. This means the oxygen escapes and the sediment and minerals sink to the bottom, resulting in a block of ice that is about 75 per cent clear, and the cloudy 25 per cent you can cut off and dispose of.

TECHNIQUES

Technique is very important when it comes to making drinks. With practice your drinks will continue to improve, "Kaizen"...

HOW TO USE
A JIGGER AND CHEF SPOONS

o

In our opinion, it's important to measure out all your ingredients with a jigger to ensure consistency. Always fill to the correct line on the jigger, or until the liquid is completely level on a chef spoon to yield a great finished product.

HOW TO USE
A TWO-PIECE SHAKER

o

When shaking, you are mixing and chilling the drink, while also allowing for a controlled amount of dilution. In a two-piece shaker, we prefer to "build" (see pages 23–24) all the ingredients in the small tin and to place the ice in the large tin. Our maxim is the more ice, the better, and so we recommend filling this tin as full as possible. Next, upend the small tin so you pour the ingredients over the ice, and seal the shaker with a firm tap. If you use this method, you can be much more consistent with the outcome of your shake, taking into consideration; temperature, lack of loss of ingredients and dilution.

When closing a two-piece shaker, you get the best results if the sides of the small tin and large tin are aligned. When looking down, try to align where the tins touch on the side furthest from you, or in the 12 o'clock position, which means the part of the tins where you want to hit is at a 120-degree angle, or at the 4 o'clock position. This should mean that the tins open easily after you have shaken.

When shaking, hold the top of the small tin with your dominant hand and the bottom of the large tin with your weaker hand, as this should keep them firmly together while you are shaking. Shake as hard as you can for the desired time, as the harder you shake, the better the results. Always make sure that you face the bottom and top of the shaker away from your guests and also the bottles on a back bar, just in case you let go. It happens, and it is never pretty.

And a final word of warning: never place anything with carbonation inside your shaker!

HOW TO USE
A THREE-PIECE
SHAKER

o

First, place all your ingredients in the base of the shaker, fill two-thirds with ice and add the lid. Wait and allow your shaker to "breathe" for a moment, before gently placing on the cap. Hold in your hands with your thumb on the cap but without pressing your whole hand against the tin – you want as little contact as possible with your warm skin while still being able to hold it firmly. Shake in a robust manner. Remove the cap and strain into your glass.

Please note, any drink that requires you to shake with fresh fruit or herbs will work much better in a two-piece shaker, as otherwise the strainer on a three-piece will become blocked.

HOW TO
DRY SHAKE

o

The previous two techniques are "wet" shakes; when you shake all the ingredients together with ice before serving. A "dry" shake is an extra step that is done before a "wet" shake and is used for drinks that contain egg white. Shaking the ingredients together first without any ice creates a beautiful foam on the top of the drink which wouldn't be achieved with only a "wet" shake. However, it only really works with a two-piece shaker, as with a three-piece it can result in spillage and an ineffective result as the seal is less secure. Some people swear by the "Reverse Dry Shake" where you shake your egg white drink with ice first, then remove the ice and shake again. We prefer not to use this method as it creates a foam that is too fluffy and some of the ingredients can be lost.

Alternatively, you could also use a hand blender to blend your ingredients before "wet" shaking, which is a fast and effective way of skipping the "dry" shake step if necessary.

To "dry" shake, add all the ingredients except the egg to your to shaker, then add the egg at the last minute. It is important to do it in this order as otherwise the acid in the citrus can start to "cook" the proteins in the egg. Place the small part of your shaker directly in the middle of the large shaker. Remember last time we wanted the sides to touch? This time we don't want any of them to be aligned – the small half of the shaker should sit directly in the middle of the large half. Shake for 10 seconds in a vertical motion, as the up and down movement really helps to break up and foam the egg white.

Finish the drink off with a "wet" shake using ice to complete the preparation of the cocktail. This should result in a beautifully smooth and fluffy "foam" on top of your drink.

HOW TO STIR

○

Stirring achieves something similar to a shake – mixing, chilling and dilution – but introduces less aeration and so results in a drink with a silky texture and smoother mouthfeel. The best technique is to add your ingredients to a mixing tin, top up with ice and stir as quickly as your hands allow. If possible, hold the mixing vessel around the top rim as this minimizes any transfer of heat from your hands, and your wrist should not move and all of the hard work should be done with your fingers. The faster you stir, the better.

HOW TO BUILD

○

When you "build" you are creating the drink inside the glass in which it is served. There is much less dilution with this method and therefore all the ingredients should be stored in the fridge. Place them in the bottom of the glass and gently stir with a bar spoon, then add your ice and stir gently again.

Drinks that are topped up, for example with soda water, tonic water, etc. are slightly different. We recommend placing your ingredients in the bottom of the glass, stirring gently and then topping up. If possible, pour the soda water directly onto the liquid as this will result in fewer bubbles being popped and a much more effervescent drink. Next, delicately insert your bar spoon and lift up the ice three times to help disperse the liquids evenly throughout the drink.

HOW TO THROW

○

This is a very theatrical way of preparing a drink and is when you pour the contents from one vessel into another vessel, generally from a great height. The aeration creates lots of little bubbles and so produces a wonderfully textured drink. However, it is not such a great method for cocktails made with citrus as it can cause the drink to taste a little flat. It's also not as effective for lowering the temperature of the cocktail.

We don't use this method too much, but we do like it for a Bellini, and find a two-piece shaker works very well. Two larger shaker tins could also be used as it may be a little easier to start with. Place your ingredients in the small tin and fill the large tin about two-thirds full with ice and fit a strainer on top to keep this in place. Ideally, this should nestle snugly into the large tin to keep the ice in place, as well as allowing liquid to flow through quite smoothly.

Add your liquid into the large tin, and pass back and forth several times. Ideally, your large tin should be as far above your head as possible and the small tin the furthest distance away that you can manage. The liquid should fall nice and slowly in a vertical motion into your small tin below. Start with the containers quite close together and then move the catching vessel further and further down to elongate the throw.

HOW TO SWIZZLE

○

Similar to when you build a drink, "swizzling" is done in the same vessel in which a cocktail is served and should always be performed with a swizzle stick. This is a small stick with little holes in it that will either remove the bubbles in a fizzy drink or froth up a still one. However, if one is not available, a bar spoon will suffice.

When making a Swizzle, the technique is, when your ingredients are in the glass and you've topped up with crushed ice, to insert the swizzle stick or spoon and hold it between the palms of your hands. Then gently rub your palms together and "swizzle" for about 7 seconds, before topping up with crushed ice and serving immediately.

HOW TO MUDDLE

○

Muddling is all about mixing and smashing herbs and fruit or other ingredients with sugar in order to extract their maximum flavour. As most cocktails that require muddling need a shake too, it's best to place your fruit in the bottom of a small shaker tin as this provides a nice stable base. Next, add your sugar syrup and, while firmly holding the tin, use a muddler (a pestle-type instrument) to pound the ingredients until they have broken down and released their flavours. The sugar syrup helps create a liquid base and also helps to extract the flavour from the ingredients.

HOW TO STRAIN/FINE-STRAIN

○

When straining from a mixing glass or tin, it is best to use a smaller Hawthorne or Julep strainer. The strainer should be held back with your index finger while the rest of your hand supports the vessel in which you mixed. The strainer should sit at a 45-degree angle on top of your ice and you should try to strain as quickly as possible to avoid over-dilution.

Martinis, Manhattans and drinks of a similar ilk should always look undisturbed and tranquil, so for these, it is best to strain down the side of the glass as this way you can avoid air bubbles from forming. If you are using high-quality ice, there is no need to fine-strain a stirred cocktail. However, you might want to remove unwanted shards of ice, which can lead to excessive dilution.

After you have shaken your cocktail in a two-piece shaker, retain all the liquid and ice in the large part of the tin and, holding a Hawthorne strainer at a 45-degree angle, strain in a similar fashion to the mixing tin. Here, you can use your other free hand to hold the fine strainer and remove any shards of ice and/or fresh ingredients. If the liquid is struggling to come through the fine strainer, use the side of the tin to tap the strainer as this will encourage the liquid to flow much more rapidly.

We recommend conical strainers for a fine strainer, as this encourages the liquid to move quickly and the tip of the cone directs the flow to a focused point.

With a three-piece shaker, you will still need to use a fine strainer to get desired results as the built in strainer is more akin to the Hawthorne or julep.

One school of thought says that egg white drinks and Espresso Martini/Vodka Espressos do not need to be fine-strained. However, we think that you achieve a better texture if you do.

Any ice shaken with fresh fruit or ingredients should be thrown straight in the bin after being shaken. Trust us, your sinks will thank you for it later!

TIMINGS

○

All our recipes are quite specific about the techniques used for their preparation and the timings that are best for their execution, and so we find the below a really useful rule of thumb:

Quick Shake – 5 Seconds

Medium Shake – 7 Seconds

Long Shake – 10 Seconds

Quick Stir – 5 Seconds

Medium Stir – 10 Seconds

Long Stir – 15 Seconds

However, there are of course a number of variables when making a drink, so you also have to bear the following in mind.

Drinks served without ice can be stirred/shaken for a little longer as they are not exposed to secondary dilution. Therefore, they will also benefit from a slightly longer chill during the preparation.

Drinks served on ice can be stirred/shaken a little less as they will be sat on ice for some time, which will in turn dilute the flavours.

Drinks topped up with soda, Champagne or anything else need even less stirring/shaking, to allow all the other wonderful ingredients to shine through.

WASH LINES

○

This is a term used to describe the level of liquid in a glass and is a very reliable indicator of whether the drink has been made properly. If you have over- or under-shaken, or incorrectly poured the ingredients or missed an ingredient, the wash line will tell you.

Most drinks should have a small gap or "window" between the liquid and the top of the glass. Not only does this make the drink look more attractive, but it also makes it easier to carry and for people to drink out of. However, if the cocktail has been shaken for too long, the wash line will be right at the top and lead to spills. There are of course a couple of exceptions, and sours or anything with cream can get away with being poured right up to the rim as the density of the ingredients helps keep the liquid inside the glass.

1.　　2.　　3.

4.　　5.　　6.　　7.

8.　　9.　　10.　　11.　　12.

13.　　14.　　15.　　16.

GARNISHES

Garnishes should always be as fresh as possible, so we recommend you make them just before preparing your drink. If they're ready, you don't have to waste time once the drink is made and you can serve everything fresh, without excessive dilution and without the temperature of the drink changing for the worse.

As a rule, we try to use as few straws as possible with our cocktails. Anything served straight up should certainly not have one but also, if a drink is served with block ice, it really doesn't need one as the closer you can get to the drink, the more you can experience its aromas and flavours. However, when we do use straws, we prefer metallic ones, which can be re-used, and we make sure we place it next to the garnish to maximize the aromas. Also, note that the straw and garnish should always be facing the person you serve the drink to.

ANGOSTURA BITTERS STRIPE

To do this, hold a bitters bottle and, in one smooth motion, run along the top of your sour glass. The drops give the drink a beautiful, complex aroma and it disguises the smell of an egg-white drink, which some people have an issue with. (See Pisco Sour, page 174)

CANDIED GINGER

Pierce a piece of candied ginger with two toothpicks and affix this to the side of your glass. (3)

CELERY STICK

Make sure both ends of your celery are trimmed with a sharp knife and that it sits just above the rim of your glass, so your guests can eat it without getting their fingers dirty. (12)

CHERRIES

When using cherries, it is always worth rinsing them before putting them in your drink. They are often preserved in a thick syrup and this can alter the balance of flavours, as well as bringing an unsightly sticky texture to the bottom of your cocktail. (2)

COFFEE BEANS

Apparently three is a lucky number for a bartender, symbolizing health, wealth and happiness. Hence, we like three Coffee beans on our Espresso Martinis. (9)

CRUSTA GLASS

Wet the outside top 2cm (½in) of the flute with a fresh lemon slice and cover with granulated sugar. Add a long lemon peel inside the glass. (See Brandy Crusta, page 72)

GRATED NUTMEG OR TONKA BEAN

Take a microplane and fine-grate your spice to a fine powder. The breaking down of the ingredient will add a beautiful aroma and subtle flavour to your cocktail. (16)

LEMON OR ORANGE COIN

A coin is a small circular piece of peel that is used to garnish drinks that are straight up.

When served without ice, drinks require more delicate aromatics in their garnish. A small coin that floats on top of the liquid won't infuse it, and will therefore give the drinker the opportunity to enjoy the nuanced flavours of the drink itself; such as in a Martini.

However, you can release the oils in the peel to give a stronger aromatic hit. To release the oils, face your peel toward your drink and gently squeeze between your index finger and thumb. If you look closely enough, you should be able to see the oils being expressed.

To make a coin, use a sharp knife to cut a shape that is roughly the size of a 10p piece, or of a "quarter", for our friends from across the pond. (4 & 6)

LEMON OR ORANGE TWIST

A twist is a long, straight piece peel used for cocktails served over ice. These drinks present a larger surface area of liquid, and also benefits from being infused with the flavour of the garnish more than a straight up cocktail.

An efficient way of creating long twists is with a Swiss-style Y-shaped peeler. It should be just slightly longer than the diameter of the glass. These allow you to get just enough pith to hold your peel in shape but not too much, which would introduce excessive bitterness.

We never rub peel around the rim of a glass as this causes the oil to stick to your lips and may affect the flavour of your next drink, and the one after that, etc. Because whoever settled with just one cocktail? (13 & 15)

LEMON OR ORANGE SLICE

These should be cut roughly 6mm (¼in) thick, and so that you can see all the segments inside. They should also be free from any pips! (8 & 10)

LIME WHEEL

Lime wheels should be cut roughly 6mm (¼in) in thickness, and be a beautiful circle. (14)

MINT SPRIG

Make sure that the mint is fresh and the stalk is trimmed to as close to the leaves as possible. (1)

OLIVES

We prefer to use Sicilian Nocellara olives as they have a wonderful buttery flavour and texture and work wonders in a Martini. (11)

PINEAPPLE WEDGE

A wedge roughly about 7mm (¼in) thick should do nicely here. (7)

SALT RIM

Wet just the rim of a coupette glass with a fresh lime wedge and gently cover in coarse sea salt. The width of the salt rim should be about 3mm (⅛in). We prefer to use sea salt flakes, which we crush with a mortar and pestle. They have a better flavour and texture and, due to less surface coverage, the salt is much more palatable. In the same way as the sugar rim, try not to get any salt on the inside of the glass as it will change the flavour and unbalance the drink.

SHREDDED ORANGE PEEL

There are two options here, either using a canal knife or a sharp knife. Run the sharp knife along the orange peel to create a thin and elegant shape. (5)

SOURS AND ESPRESSO MARTINI SPRAY

A great way to get a clean and smooth foam on top of your sours and espresso martinis is by using an atomizer. Fill one with either vodka/gin, depending on your spirit base, and spray a couple of times over your cocktail. This helps to pop the bubbles on top of your egg white or foam, resulting in a perfect looking sour.

SUGAR RIM

Wet just the rim of a coupette glass with a fresh lemon slice and gently cover in granulated sugar. The width of the sugar rim should be about 2mm (¹/₁₆in). Try not to get any sugar on the inside of the glass as it will change the flavour and unbalance the drink. A little trick we learnt recently is that using a pastry brush and sugar syrup instead of fresh lemon is a great way to create an elegant sugar rim.

RECIPES FOR PREPARATIONS

CITRUS JUICE

Many of the recipes in this book call for fresh citrus juice. We find that the best kind comes from a citrus press as it also extracts the oils from the peel, resulting in a much more aromatic juice. However, fresh juice starts to oxidize straight away, so please store in airtight containers in the fridge and throw away after six hours for maximum freshness.

For limes and lemons, we also recommend adding salt straight after pressing as this helps preserve the quality, as well as enhancing the flavour. Take 1 litre of fresh juice and add 1g of sea salt. However, don't add salt to grapefruit or orange juice, as these are often added to drinks along with lemon or lime juice and so would result in the flavour becoming overly salty.

SUGAR SYRUP

1kg (2lb 3oz) Granulated Sugar
500ml (17fl oz) Water

○

Place both ingredients in a bowl and stir to dissolve the sugar. Use hot water or a whisk for quicker results. We prefer a 2:1 syrup, or 2 parts sugar to 1 part water as this keeps the amount of water and the amount of dilution low.

HONEY SYRUP

3 Parts Honey
1 Part Hot Water

○

Place both ingredients in a bowl and stir to dissolve the honey. Store in the fridge once cooled.

BROWN SUGAR SYRUP

1kg (2lb 3oz) Brown Sugar
500ml (17fl oz) Water

○

Made in the same way as Sugar Syrup (see left).

EGG WHITE/YOLKS

Separate the egg whites and yolks. With a sharp knife, "chop up" the egg whites or yolks and store in squeezy bottles. Keep refrigerated and throw away after one day. The chopping up helps you have whites/yolks that are much easier to measure in a jigger.

PASSION FRUIT SYRUP

5 Fresh Passion Fruits
500g (17½ oz) Granulated Sugar
250ml (8½fl oz) Water

○

Remove the pulp and seeds from 5 passion fruit, mix with granulated sugar and set aside for 30 minutes. Add the water and stir to dissolve the sugar and passion fruit mix. Set aside for 24 hours and then strain through a fine strainer. Bottle and store in the fridge.

GRENADINE SYRUP

250ml (8½fl oz) Pomegranate Juice
500g (17½ oz) Granulated Sugar

○

Place both ingredients in a bowl and stir to dissolve the sugar. Bottle and store in the fridge.

GINGER SYRUP

4 Parts Ginger Juice
3 Parts Granulated Sugar

○

Pass "old" ginger through a centrifugal juicer with its skin on. Mix the juice with granulated sugar and stir to dissolve. Bottle and store in the fridge.

"Old ginger" is dry and fibrous and slightly spicier than its fresh counterpart "young ginger". We prefer the flavour profile of the senior relative.

TOMATO MIX

500ml (17fl oz) Tomato Juice
400ml (13½fl oz) Tomato Passata

○

Mix both ingredients together and bottle and store in the fridge.

ACIDIC ORANGE JUICE

5g (⅙oz) Citric Acid
250ml (8½fl oz) Fresh Orange Juice

○

Dissolve the citric acid into the orange juice. Bottle and store in the fridge.

VANILLA CREAM

250ml (8½fl oz) Double Cream
5ml (⅙fl oz) Vanilla Essence

○

Mix both ingredients together, bottle and store in the fridge. The strength of vanilla essence can vary, so adjust to taste.

DEFINITIONS

The brands we have listed in this book are brands that we love and the drinks we use them in are all down to our own choice and preference. We took into consideration price point, global availability, consistency and, most importantly, flavour and quality. However, taste is such a personal thing that you might prefer the subtle differences of an alternative brand and, as these are interchangeable, please do swap away. Likewise, our contributors have chosen their spirits in the same way and we trust their judgement.

ABSINTHE

A spirit high in ABV made from wormwood, anise, fennel and other medicinal herbs. Sometimes referred to as "The Green Fairy".

Pernod Absinthe, La Fee Parisienne, Jade 1901, Vieux Pontarlier

AGRICOLE RUM (OR RHUM AGRICOLE)

This is the French word for rum that is distilled from cane juice rather than molasses, and originally came from the French Caribbean islands.

Trois Rivières VSOP, Trois Rivières Blanc

AMARETTO

An almond-flavoured liqueur that comes from Saronno, Italy.

Luxardo Amaretto di Saschira, Saliza Amaretto

PICON AMER

A bittersweet orange-flavoured French aperitif.

ANGOSTURA BITTERS

One of the must-have ingredients for any bar. Distilled from gentian, herbs and spices, it has a complex and, of course, bitter flavour and comes from the House of Angostura in Trinidad and Tobago.

APEROL

An Italian apéritif made from gentian, rhubarb and orange, among other different ingredients. Is it time for an Aperol Spritz yet?

APPLEJACK

An apple brandy from the USA.

Laird's Applejack

APRICOT BRANDY

A sweet apricot-flavoured liqueur that is based on grape brandy.

Merlet Lune d'Abricot

BÉNÉDICTINE D.O.M

A French liqueur flavoured with numerous herbs and spices.

BOURBON

A barrel-aged American whiskey made predominantly from corn, with the rest made up of wheat, rye and barley.

Woodford Reserve, Elijah Craig 12, Four Roses Single Barrel, Bulleit, Michter's US*1 Bourbon, Maker's Mark, Basil Hayden's

CACHAÇA

A spirit made from sugar cane juice. Predominantly produced and served in Brazil.

Yaguara, Abelha

CALVADOS

A French apple brandy from Normandy.

Christian Drouin Selection Coeur de Lion, Dupont

CAMPARI

A bitter, dark red Italian aperitif, made from fruits, herbs and plants. A must for the Negroni and Boulevardier cocktails.

CHAMPAGNE

A sparkling wine from the Champagne region in France.

Perrier-Jouët Grand Brut NV, Charles Heidsieck Brut Reserve, Ruinart Blanc de Blancs, Pol Roger Brut Réserve NV

CHERRY HEERING

A Danish-produced cherry liqueur, made to a recipe dating from 1818.

COCCHI AMERICANO

An Italian apéritif wine made from quinine, among other botanicals.

COGNAC

A French grape brandy from Cognac in France.

Hennessy V.S.O.P, Martell V.S.O.P, Pierre Ferrand 1840, Pierre Ferrand Ambre, Hine Rare V.S.O.P, D'USSÉ V.S.O.P, Remy Martin V.S.O.P

COINTREAU

An orange-flavoured liqueur from France.

COFFEE LIQUEUR

A liqueur based on, you guessed it, coffee.

Mr. Black Cold Brew Coffee Liqueur

CRÈME DE BANANE

A banana-flavoured liqueur.

Giffard Crème Banane

CRÈME DE CACAO

A chocolate-based liqueur. Can be white or brown.

Bols Crème de Cacao White, Bols Crème de Cacao Brown, Giffard Crème de Cacao

CRÈME DE CASSIS

A liqueur made from blackcurrants, essential for making a Kir or Kir Royale.

Merlet Crème de Cassis

CRÈME DE MENTHE

A liqueur made from mint. Available in white or green.

Briottet Menthe Blanche, Briottet Menthe Verte

CRÈME DE MÛRE

A fruit liqueur made from blackberries.

Merlet Crème de Mûre

CRÈME DE PAMPLEMOUSSE

A grapefruit-based liqueur.

Briottet Pamplemousse Rose

CRÈME DE PÊCHE

A peach flavoured liqueur.

Merlet Crème de Pêche

CRÈME DE VIOLETTE

A floral and violet-coloured liqueur made from... violets.

The Bitter Truth Violet Liqueur

CURAÇAO

A liqueur made from the dried peel of Laraha citrus fruit, grown on the Caribbean island of Curaçao.

Pierre Ferrand Dry Curaçao

DRAMBUIE

A golden-coloured Scotch whisky made with honey, herbs and spices.

DRY VERMOUTH

A fortified white wine made from various botanicals, such as cloves, cinnamon, quinine, citrus peel, cardamom, marjoram, chamomile, coriander, juniper, hyssop and ginger.

Noilly Prat Original

DUBONNET

A brand of sweet aromatized wine – an apéritif.

FALERNUM

A Caribbean syrup liqueur flavoured with lime and also containing other spices. Essential in many Tiki drinks.

FERNET BRANCA

A brand of amaro, which is a bitter aromatic spirit made from a plethora of different herbs and roots; a common Italian digestif.

FINO SHERRY

A dry and complex sherry from Spain.

Tio Pepe

GALLIANO L'AUTENTICO

A sweet vanilla-based herbal liqueur from Italy.

GIN

A juniper-based spirit that also includes numerous other botanicals. Gin is an incredibly fast growing category, with many different styles.

Tanqueray, Tanqueray No. Ten, Cotswolds, Monkey 47, Chase GB, Bombay Sapphire, Star of Bombay, No.3, Beefeater, Beefeater 24, Portobello Road, Plymouth, Sipsmith, Fords, Gin Mare, Old Young's 1829, Ki No Bi, Jensen's Old Tom, Citadelle Original, Hepple, Hendrick's

GINGER ALE & GINGER BEER

Ginger-flavoured soft drinks. Ginger ale tends to be a little softer and less spicy.

Schweppes Ginger Ale

GRAND MARNIER CORDON ROUGE

A brandy-based orange liqueur from France.

CHARTREUSE GREEN

A French herbal liqueur originally made by Carthusian monks to a recipe set out in a manuscript from 1605. Distilled from 130 different herbs and botanicals.

IRISH WHISKEY

This is whiskey produced in Ireland. It can be based on malted or unmalted barley, or both, and tends to be triple-distilled.

Jameson, Redbreast 12

LILLET BLANC

A golden-coloured aromatized wine, made with quinine and other botanicals. A popular French apéritif.

MADEIRA

A fortified wine made on the Portuguese Madeira Islands.

MARASCHINO

A liqueur made from Marasca cherries.

Luxardo Maraschino Originale

MASTIHA

A liqueur made from the resin of the mastic tree, a small Mediterranean evergreen, and flavoured with pine or cedar-like notes.

Skinos Mastiha

MEZCAL

A spirit native to Mexico, made from wild agave. Tends to be quite smoky in character.

Del Maguey Vida, Del Maguey Chichicapa, Montelobos Joven

OLOROSO SHERRY

A style of sherry from Spain, quite nutty and with flavours of dried fruit.

Gonzalez Byass

ORANGE BITTERS

A form of bitters that utilizes orange peel for its bitter flavour and combines it with other spices, such as cardamom, caraway seed and coriander.

Regans' Orange Bitters No.6

PALO CORTADO

A delicate and aromatic style of sherry from Spain.

Gonzalez Byass

PEDRO XIMENEZ

A very sweet, syrupy, dark style of sherry from Spain.

Gonzalez Byass

PEYCHAUD'S BITTERS

Created by Antoine Amédée Peychaud, this is a gentian-based bitter, combined with anise and mint, and is an absolute necessity for the Sazerac cocktail.

PIMM'S NO.1 CUP

A gin-based fruit cup from England.

PISCO

A grape brandy, originating in Chile and Peru.

La Caravedo

PORT

A sweet fortified wine from Portugal.

Dow's

ROSATO VERMOUTH

This sits comfortably between dry and sweet vermouths in terms of its flavour profile.

Martini Rosato

RUM

A spirit made from sugarcane byproducts, such as molasses or sugarcane juice.

Mount Gay XO, Havana Club Seleccion De Maestros, Havana Club Especial, Havana Club 3, Diplomatico Exclusiva Reserva, Bacardi Ron Superior Heritage, Bacardi 8, Bacardi Carta Blanca, Bacardi Añejo Cuatro, Gosling's Black Seal, Gosling's Black Seal 151, Appleton Estate Reserve 8 Year Old, Plantation 3 Stars, Myers's, El Dorado 12, Appleton Estate V/X, Banks 7 Golden Age, Caña Brava, The Duppy Share

RYE

A whiskey derived predominantly from the rye grain.

Sazerac Straight Rye, Lot 40, Woodford Reserve Rye, Michter's US*1 Straight Rye

SCOTCH

A malt or grain whisky made in Scotland.

Chivas Regal 12, Auchentoshan Three Wood, Monkey Shoulder, Dewar's 12, The Macallan 12 Year Old Double Cask, Lagavulin 16, Johnnie Walker Black Label, The Balvenie DoubleWood 12, Glenfiddich 12

SLOE GIN

A liqueur made from infusing sloes (the fruit of the blackthorn) in gin.

Monkey 47 Sloe Gin, Plymouth Sloe Gin

SODA WATER

Water that is made fizzy with carbon dioxide – carbonated.

Schweppes Soda Water

SUZE

A gentian-based French brand of apéritif.

SWEET VERMOUTH

A sweet fortified wine flavoured with various botanicals, but must include wormwood.

Asterley Bros. Estate English Vermouth, Cocchi Storico Vermouth di Torino, Punt e Mes, Martini Rosso

TONIC WATER

A carbonated soda flavoured lightly with quinine.

Schweppes Indian Tonic Water

TEQUILA

A Mexican spirit made specifically from the blue agave plant, primarily in the region surrounding the city of Tequila.

Tapatio Blanco, Herradura Plata Blanco, Ocho Blanco, Ocho Reposado, Partida Reposado, Olmeca Altos Reposado, Olmeca Altos Blanco, L&J Blanco

VODKA

A clear distilled spirit that is quite nuanced in flavour and aroma. Traditionally, it was made from fermented cereal grains or potatoes, but these days fruits or sugar can also be the base.

Belvedere, Absolut Citron, Absolut Elyx, Absolut Orginal, Grey Goose, Grey Goose Citron, Potocki, Reyka, Ketel One

GLOSSARY

ABV	Alcohol By Volume.
AGAVE SYRUP	A sweetener made from the agave plant.
APERITIF	A drink designed to stimulate the appetite.
AMARO	A style of Italian liqueur flavoured with herbs and botanicals.
CHURN	Using a spoon to mix liquid, crushed ice and other ingredients in a glass.
CITRIC ACID	An acid derived from citrus fruit.
COCO LÓPEZ	A tinned coconut cream.
CORDIAL	Essentially a syrup with a form of acid.
DIGESTIF	A drink to aid digestion.
DRY SHAKE	Shaking without ice to help the inclusion of egg or dairy drinks.
FLOAT	Adding liquid to sit on top of a drink.
FREE POUR	Pouring liquid without the use of a measure.
GARNISH	The decorative flourish on a cocktail.
NAKED	Served without a garnish.
NEAT	Served without ice.
OLEO SACCHARUM	A combination of oil and sugar, typically a syrup.
ON THE ROCKS	Served over ice.
ORANGE FLOWER WATER	Flavoured water derived from orange blossoms.
ORGEAT	An almond and orange flower water syrup.
PREMIX	A mix of ingredients ready to pour.
SORBET	A frozen sweetened water product.
STRAIGHT UP	Served without ice in a cocktail glass.
TONKA BEAN	A fragrant ingredient from Central and South America.
WET SHAKE	Shaking with ice. Tends to be post dry shake if specified.

THE
DRINKS

ADONIS

Created around the mid-1880s in honour of the Broadway musical of the same name – the first, in fact, to run for more than 500 performances – the Adonis is a true classic of the American cocktail bar.

We like to add a touch of sugar syrup as sugar is a great flavour carrier and works well here, enhancing the relatively subtle sherry and vermouth. You won't find this extra touch of sweetness in traditional versions of the drink, but we like how it underscores all the flavour notes. Additionally, we prefer to use Oloroso Sherry instead of the more traditional Fino, as it plays well with the other ingredients. The sweet complexity of the Oloroso adds much more to the drink.

30ml (1fl oz) Oloroso Sherry - Gonzalez Byass
30ml (1fl oz) Sweet Vermouth - Asterley Bros. Estate English Vermouth
1.25ml (2 dashes) Orange Bitters - Regans' Orange Bitters No. 6
2.5ml (4 dashes) Sugar Syrup

Glassware: Coupette
Ice: Served Without
Garnish: Orange Coin
Preparation: Long Stir

o

Add all the ingredients to a mixing glass with ice and stir.
Strain into a coupette, garnish with an orange coin and serve.

Tip: For an alternative drink in a similar style, try the Bamboo –
30ml (1fl oz) Fino Sherry, 30ml (1fl oz) Dry Vermouth, 2 dashes of Orange Bitters, 1 dash of Angostura Bitters, 2.5ml (4 dashes) Sugar Syrup and garnished with a lemon coin.

AIRMAIL

First appearing in print in 1949, in *Esquire Magazine's Handbook for Hosts*, the Airmail is a very elegant drink. We prefer to serve it in a champagne flute rather than a highball glass, to emphasize this quality and also to keep the drink effervescent.

As with all drinks that are topped up with champagne, make sure the shake is quite short, as this keeps the dilution low and the flavour intense.

30ml (1fl oz) Aged Rum – Havana Club Especial
15ml (½fl oz) Lime Juice
15ml (½fl oz) Honey Syrup
Top Champagne – Perrier-Jouët Grand Brut NV

Glassware: Champagne Flute
Ice: Served Without
Garnish: Served Without
Preparation: Quick Shake, Top with Champagne

○

Add the rum, lime juice and honey syrup to a shaker with ice.

Shake, then strain into a champagne flute.

Top up with Champagne, stir gently to mix and serve.

AMARETTO SOUR

Like many cocktails, it's impossible to trace the exact origins of the Amaretto Sour. However, it's been a classic for quite some time now and its unique sweet–sour notes combine to make an indisputably sophisticated drink.

We like to use a very small amount of sugar as Amaretto is quite sweet, and so only a little bit is necessary to keep the flavours balanced. As with other sours, we prefer to serve in a coupette glass and to add our bitters on top as this helps to cover up the subtle smell of egg white and the bitters add a nice complex aroma. We prefer to serve this straight up to limit dilution and to make a more flavoursome drink.

50ml (1¾oz) Amaretto - Luxardo Amaretto di Saschira
25ml (⅘fl oz) Lemon Juice
25ml (⅘fl oz) Egg White
5ml (⅙fl oz) Sugar Syrup

Glassware: Coupette
Ice: Served Without
Preparation: Dry Shake and Long Wet Shake
Garnish: Angostura Bitter Stripe

o

Add all the ingredients to a shaker and dry shake (see page 23). Add ice and wet shake (see page 23). Strain into a chilled coupette, garnish with a bitters stripe and serve.

AMERICANO

Spawned from the famous Milano Torino – a drink of Campari and sweet vermouth created at Milan's Caffè Camparino in the 1860s – the Americano came about due to the American tourists who liked to drink theirs with a little extra soda. In our opinion, the soda adds a nice carbonated texture, but you only need a touch so as to keep the flavour of the other ingredients nice and robust. We also like to use a discarded orange coin (see page 29) for aroma, while the orange slice flavours the cocktail ever so slightly.

When topping up with soda, the best way is to pour slowly and to then very gently lift the ice cube with a bar spoon to mix the liquids of different densities – that way you don't pop as many bubbles.

50ml (1¾fl oz) Campari
50ml (1¾fl oz) Sweet Vermouth - Cocchi Storico Vermouth di Torino
Top Soda - Schweppes Soda

Glassware: Highball
Ice: Block Ice
Garnish: Orange Slice and Discarded Orange Coin
Preparation: Build and Top With Soda

○

Add the Campari and sweet vermouth to a chilled highball glass with ice.
Top with a small amount of soda, then gently stir. Add the orange slice
and gently squeeze an orange coin over the top. Serve.

Tip: Instead of soda, try topping up with a little Prosecco to create a Negroni Sbagliato.

APEROL SPRITZ

Derived from the Spritz Veneziano, a combination of wine, bitter liqueur and sparkling mineral water, which gained widespread popularity in the early 1900s with the advent of carbonated drinks, this is also quite similar in DNA to the Americano. Some people may question why we don't add soda but, in our opinion, as you already have the fizziness or "bead" from the prosecco, there is nothing that the soda adds, it only takes away and we much prefer not to dilute.

We also prefer to serve in a rocks glass as, when ice is added to stemware, condensation starts to run down the base and then onto the person drinking it.

50ml (1¾fl oz) Aperol
100ml (3½fl oz) Prosecco

Glassware: Rocks Glass
Ice: Block Ice
Garnish: Orange Slice and Discarded Orange Coin
Preparation: Build

o

Add both ingredients to a chilled rocks glass with ice and gently stir. Add the orange slice and gently squeeze an orange coin over the top. Serve.

ARMY & NAVY

The recipe for an Army & Navy cocktail first appeared in print in 1948 in *The Fine Art of Mixing Drinks* by David Embury, known to many as "The Escoffier of cocktail books".

Small Hands Orgeat, an artisanal almond syrup made with apricot kernels, is an incredible product with a delicate marzipan and floral citrus flavour. It contains far less sugar than many other syrups, so you need to use a fairly large measure for this cocktail. The Orgeat should create a nice layer of bubbles on top of the drink, so don't be tempted to drop the lemon peel into the drink as this will burst them and ruin the presentation.

50ml (1¾fl oz) Gin – Tanqueray Gin
25ml (⅘fl oz) Lemon Juice
20ml (¾fl oz) Orgeat – Small Hands Orgeat

Glassware: Coupette
Ice: Served Without
Garnish: Discarded Lemon Coin
Preparation: Long Shake

○

Add all the ingredients to a shaker with ice and shake.

Strain into a chilled coupette, gently squeeze a lemon coin over the top and then serve.

AVIATION

This recipe was first published in Hugo R. Ensslin's *Recipes for Mixed Drinks*, published in 1916, and many believe it came from the time when he was head bartender at The Hotel Wallick in New York. Essentially, it is a Gin Sour with a couple of extra layers of flavour.

For any cocktail that is garnished with a cherry, we always recommend you wash the cherry first. Maraschino cherries are coated in a rich syrup and this will alter the balance and appearance of a drink unless removed. Our preferred brand is Luxardo as these cherries contain only natural ingredients, with no preservatives or thickeners.

35ml (1¼fl oz) Gin - Cotswolds Dry Gin
25ml (⅘fl oz) Lemon Juice
7.5ml (¼fl oz) Violet Liqueur - The Bitter Truth Violet Liqueur
7.5ml (¼fl oz) Maraschino - Luxardo Maraschino
7.5ml (¼fl oz) Sugar Syrup

Glassware: Coupette
Ice: Served Without
Garnish: Washed Maraschino Cherry
Preparation: Long Shake

o

Add all the ingredients to a shaker with ice and shake.
Strain into a chilled coupette, garnish with a cherry and serve.

THE BEE'S KNEES

This deliciously clean and elegant drink is thought to come from the Prohibition era in the United States (1920–1933). As it's so simple to make, you can play with the sweet/citrusy balance to suit your tastes.

The Bee's Knees was appreciated by the late, great Sasha Petraske, and he created a delicious variation by simply switching the lemon juice for lime – he named it The Business. Sasha is widely credited as being the instigator of our current renaissance in cocktails. He is still a huge inspiration to us and thousands of bartenders around the world. If it weren't for him, the cocktail scene would not be what it is today.

50ml (1¾fl oz) Gin – Monkey 47 Dry Gin
25ml (⅘fl oz) Lemon Juice
15ml (½fl oz) Honey Syrup

Glassware: Coupette
Ice: Served Without
Garnish: Served Without
Preparation: Long Shake

○

Add all the ingredients to a shaker with ice and shake.
Strain into a chilled coupette and serve.

BELLINI

The Bellini is quite simply stroke of genius – using deliciously sweet Italian peaches to flavour a glass of prosecco – and was created in 1945 by Giuseppe Cipriani at Harry's Bar in Venice. He then named this peachy pink drink after the Italian Renaissance painter Giovanni Bellini, who was known for his predominantly pink paintings.

Harry's is one of the world's most legendary bars, located on Piazza San Marco. If you are planning a trip to Venice, try to visit between May and September, as this is when the legendary white peaches are in season.

We prefer to "throw" our Bellinis, a technique used to chill and mix before serving, as we find the slight dilution and aerations created really help to open up the drink and create a much smoother cocktail. The throwing also helps to disperse some of the bubbles in the prosecco and gives you a much silkier mouthfeel – like drinking velvet. If fresh white peaches are also in season, this kind of Bellini is probably worlds apart from the last one you were served for brunch.

50ml (1¾fl oz) White Peach Purée
100ml (3½fl oz) Prosecco

Glassware: Fizz Glass
Ice: Served Without
Garnish: Served Without
Preparation: Throw

○

Add all the ingredients to the large part of a tin then add ice. Throw into a smaller tin three times, then pour into a chilled fizz glass and serve.

BETWEEN THE SHEETS

Many attribute this cocktail to Mr Harry MacElhone, while he was working at Harry's New York Bar in Paris during the 1930s. However, there are other claims that it was invented at The Berkeley Hotel in the 1920s, or even in French brothels, where it was served up to prostitutes as an apéritif. However, everyone can agree on the fact that it is a derivative of the Sidecar, with the addition of rum and a little less cognac.

There are plenty of recipes in circulation for this drink – some shaken, some stirred. This is our preferred one as we find it has the best balance of flavours. Complex and refreshing.

20ml (¾fl oz) Aged Rum - Mount Gay XO
20ml (¾fl oz) Cognac - Rémy Martin VSOP
10ml (⅓fl oz) Triple Sec - Cointreau
25ml (⅘fl oz) Lemon Juice
10ml (⅓fl oz) Sugar Syrup

Glassware: Coupette
Ice: Served Without
Garnish: Discarded Lemon Coin
Preparation: Long Shake

o

Add all the ingredients to a shaker with ice and shake.

Strain into a chilled coupette, gently squeeze a lemon coin over the top and then serve.

BLACK RUSSIAN

Legend has it that the Black Russian was created by Gustave Tops in the Hotel Metropole in Brussels in 1949. The drink was made as a tribute to Perle Mesta, the United States Ambassador to Luxembourg at the time, but acquired its name as the coffee liqueur was black and the vodka was Russian.

Some people like to add a little Coca-Cola to this drink – we prefer it without, as it was intended, but if requested, we are more than happy to oblige. Add 50ml (1¾fl oz) Coca-Cola and make sure all the ingredients are mixed together.

35ml (1¼fl oz) Vodka - Reyka
20ml (¾fl oz) Coffee Liqueur - Mr. Black Cold Brew Coffee Liqueur

Glassware: Rocks Glass
Ice: Block Ice
Garnish: Served Without
Preparation: Quick Stir

○

Add all the ingredients to a mixing glass with ice and stir.
Strain into a chilled rocks glass and serve.

BLOOD & SAND

It's the colours of this drink – blood red from the cherry liqueur and orange sand from the orange juice – that link it to the 1922 bullfighter movie, starring Rudolph Valentino, after which it was named. The creator of the drink is unknown, but it is included in *The Savoy Cocktail Book*, published in 1930, and has remained a bar classic ever since.

Traditionally, the drink is made up of equal parts and yet we feel it benefits from a little more zest, and so we create an orange juice with extra citric acid to bring the flavours more in balance.

25ml (⅘fl oz) Scotch - Glenfiddich 12
25ml (⅘fl oz) Cherry Brandy - Cherry Heering Liqueur
25ml (⅘fl oz) Sweet Vermouth - Cocchi Storico Vermouth di Torino
25ml (⅘fl oz) Acidic Orange Juice (see page 33)

Glassware: Coupette
Ice: Served Without
Garnish: Discarded Orange Twist
Preparation: Long Shake

o

Add all the ingredients to a shaker with ice and shake.

Strain into a chilled coupette, gently squeeze an orange twist over the top and then serve.

BLOODY MARY

There are a number of claims to the invention of the Bloody Mary. Perhaps the most credible one is Fernand Petiot's at The New York Bar in Paris during the early 1920s, which was soon to become the legendary Harry's New York Bar. And whether he invented the iconic combination of tomato juice and vodka or not, he later claimed all the credit for adding in the extras – the salt, black pepper, cayenne pepper, lemon juice and Worcestershire Sauce – which of course make it the Bloody Mary we know and love today.

We absolutely love Bloody Marys and yet we don't always enjoy the texture of tomato juice, which leaves us with a bit of a dilemma. However, to get around that, we blend a mix of passata and tomato juice, which creates a thicker texture and a flavour that is more intense on the palate. Now, it's perfect.

50ml (1¾fl oz) Vodka - Belvedere
80ml (2⅖fl oz) Tomato Mix (see page 33)
10ml (⅓fl oz) Lemon Juice
Pinch of Celery Salt
Pinch of Black Pepper
15ml (½fl oz) Worcestershire Sauce - Lea & Perrins
3 dashes of Hot Sauce - Tabasco

Glassware: Highball
Ice: Block Ice
Garnish: Trimmed Celery Stick
Preparation: Build

Add all the ingredients to a chilled highball glass, stir to mix, add ice,
garnish with a celery stick and serve.

BOBBY BURNS

Harry Cradock, in *The Savoy Cocktail Book* of 1930, describes the Bobby Burns as "One of the very best whisky cocktails and a very fast mover on Saint Andrew's Day."

In our opinion, the drink needs a touch of bitterness and so we've added a dash of Angostura, but only a very little, so as not to overpower the beautiful notes of the BÉNÉDICTINE D.O.M Liqueur.

50ml (1¾fl oz) Scotch - The Balvenie DoubleWood 12
20ml (¾fl oz) Sweet Vermouth - Cocchi Storico Vermouoth di Torino
5ml (⅙fl oz) BÉNÉDICTINE D.O.M. Liqueur
1 dash of Angostura Bitters

Glassware: Coupette
Ice: Served Without
Garnish: Lemon Coin
Preparation: Long Stir

○

Add all the ingredients to a mixing glass with ice and stir.
Strain into a chilled coupette, garnish with a lemon coin and serve.

JOE SCHOFIELD

—

WILLIAM WALLACE

50ml (1¾fl oz) Scotch – Chivas Regal 12
10ml (⅓fl oz) Pedro Ximenez – González Byass
10ml (⅓fl oz) Sweet Vermouth – Asterley Bros. Estate English Vermouth
2.5ml (4 dashes) Orange Bitters – Regans' Orange Bitters No. 6

Glassware: Coupette
Ice: Served Without
Garnish: Orange Coin
Preparation: Long Stir

o

Add all the ingredients to a mixing glass with ice and stir.

Pour into a chilled coupette, garnish with an orange coin and serve.

BOULEVARDIER

This wonderful Negroni variation is yet another fabulous creation by Harry MacElhone at Harry's New York Bar in Paris, who made it for a fellow ex-pat, Erskinne Gwynne, who at the time edited a monthly magazine called *The Boulevardier*, hence the name.

Our version calls for a little bit extra of the hero spirit, bourbon, so as the Campari and sweet vermouth don't overpower its flavour.

40ml (1⅖fl oz) Bourbon – Basil Hayden's Kentucky Straight Bourbon
20ml (¾fl oz) Sweet Vermouth – Martini Rosso
20ml (¾fl oz) Campari

Glassware: Rocks Glass
Ice: Block Ice
Garnish: Long Orange Peel
Preparation: Quick Stir

o

Add all the ingredients to a mixing glass with ice and stir.

Strain over ice into a rocks glass, garnish with orange peel and serve.

Tip: For a wonderful variation, try the Old Pal. Swap bourbon for rye, sweet vermouth for dry and serve straight up with a lemon coin.

JILLIAN VOSE

—

PSYCHO KILLER

60ml (2fl oz) Redbreast 12 Irish Whiskey
15ml (½fl oz) Giffard Banane du Brésil Liqueur
15ml (½fl oz) Giffard Crème de Cacao Blanc
20ml (¾fl oz) Campari
2 dashes of Vieux Pontarlier Absinthe

Glassware: Martini glass
Ice: Served Without
Garnish: Served Without
Preparation: Long Stir

o

Add all the ingredients to a mixing glass with ice and stir.
Pour into a chilled martini glass and serve.

BRAMBLE

Created in the mid-1980s by the celebrated Dick Bradsell at Fred's Club in Soho, London, and inspired by his childhood memories of picking blackberries on the Isle of Wight, the crème de mûre brings an interesting twist to a classic Gin Sour.

50ml (1¾fl oz) Gin – Chase GB Extra Dry Gin
25ml (⅘fl oz) Lemon Juice
10ml (⅓fl oz) Sugar Syrup
15ml (½fl oz) Crème de Mûre – Merlet Crème de Mure Sauvage

Glassware: Rocks Glass
Ice: Crushed
Garnish: 1 blackberry
Preparation: Quick Shake and Float Crème de Mûre

o

Add all the ingredients, except the crème de mûre, to a shaker with ice and shake.

Strain over crushed ice into a chilled rocks glass. Float crème de mûre on top, garnish with a blackberry and serve.

BRANDY ALEXANDER

This is a variation of an earlier gin-based cocktail (the Alexander). It was invented during the mid-1930s and has been a classic ever since. Made with cognac, dark chocolate liqueur and cream, it never fails as an indulgent after-dinner treat.

If you fancy making the original, simply swap out the cognac for gin, and we recommend also substituting the dark chocolate liqueur for white chocolate. Gin and vanilla make a great combination.

40ml (1⅖fl oz) Cognac – Pierre Ferrand 1840
20ml (¾fl oz) Crème de Cacao – Bols Crème de Cacao Brown
20ml (¾fl oz) Heavy Cream

Glassware: Coupette
Ice: Served Without
Garnish: Grated Nutmeg
Preparation: Long Shake

o

Add all the ingredients to a shaker with ice and shake.

Strain into a chilled coupette and dust with a little grated nutmeg, then serve.

BRANDY CRUSTA

This was invented around the mid-1850s by Joseph Santini at the Jewel of The South in New Orleans and, as the "first" cocktail to use fresh citrus, was quite revolutionary at the time.

The name refers to the crust of sugar and lemon peel around the rim of the glass, which is crucial to the drink and needs to be prepared in advance (see page 29). However, it's well worth the effort as this cocktail is both refreshing and complex with a beautiful pairing of citrus and Brandy. If you like it, there are many variations on this theme: Rum Crusta, Whiskey Crusta, etc.

40ml (1⅖fl oz) Cognac – Hennessy V.S.O.P
25ml (⅘fl oz) Lemon Juice
5ml (⅙fl oz) Maraschino – Luxardo Maraschino
10ml (⅓fl oz) Triple Sec – Cointreau
5ml (⅙fl oz) Sugar Syrup
1 dash of Angostura Bitters

Glassware: Champagne Flute
Ice: Served Without
Garnish: Crusta
Preparation: Long Shake

o

Add all the ingredients to a shaker with ice and shake.

Strain into a crusted champagne flute and serve.

BREAKFAST MARTINI

This was created in 1996 at The Lanesborough Hotel in London, when the legendary Italian bartender, Salvatore Calabrese, was persuaded by his wife to swap his usual breakfast of an espresso for one of toast and marmalade. A few hours later, in the Library Bar, this cocktail was born and instantly became a modern classic. This recipe is kindly provided by Salvatore himself.

50ml (1¾fl oz) Gin - Tanqueray Gin
15ml (½fl oz) Triple Sec - Cointreau
15ml (½fl oz) Lemon Juice
1 Bar Spoon (5ml or ⅙fl oz) Thin-cut Orange Marmalade

Glassware: Martini Glass
Ice: Served Without
Garnish: Shredded Orange Peel
Preparation: Long Shake

o

Add all the ingredients to a shaker and mix to incorporate the marmalade into the other ingredients. Add ice and shake.

Strain into a chilled martini glass, garnish with orange peel and serve.

BROOKLYN

In our opinion, this is a more complex, and therefore more interesting, version of a Manhattan as the dry vermouth works wonderfully to counterbalance the sweetness of the maraschino.

Created by Jacob Grohusko in New York City at the turn of the 20th century, the original version contained sweet vermouth instead of the dry vermouth we are accustomed to today. Both, however, work fantastically, so see which one suits your tastes.

50ml (1¾fl oz) Rye - Bulleit Rye Whiskey
15ml (½fl oz) Picon Amer
5ml (⅙fl oz) Maraschino - Luxardo Maraschino
5ml (⅙fl oz) Dry Vermouth - Noilly Prat Original

Glassware: Coupette
Ice: Served Without
Garnish: Cherry
Preparation: Long Stir

o

Add all the ingredients to a mixing glass with ice and stir.
Strain into a chilled coupette, garnish with a cherry and serve.

IVY MIX

—

PALO NEGRO

60ml (2fl oz) Partida Reposado Tequila
30ml (1fl oz) Lustau Palo Cortado Sherry
15ml (½fl oz) Blackstrap Rum
5ml (⅙fl oz) Grand Marnier Cordon Rouge
5ml (⅙fl oz) Demerara Syrup (see below)

Glassware: Martini glass
Ice: Served Without
Garnish: Orange Coin
Preparation: Long Stir

○

Add all the ingredients to a mixing glass with ice and stir. Pour into a chilled
martini glass, garnish with an orange coin and serve.

DEMERARA SYRUP

2 Parts Demerara Sugar
1 Part Water

○

Stir together until the sugar is dissolved.

CAIPIRINHA

The Caipirinha, the national drink of Brazil, is believed to have originated from the sugarcane-growing countryside around São Paulo in the 19th century and is now the most popular cocktail in South America – almost everyone has their own way of making it. Essential to it is the spirit cachaça, a Brazilian spirit akin to rum, which distills fresh sugarcane juice instead of molasses. Extremely simple to make and deliciously sweet, zesty and refreshing to taste. If made with vodka, the drink becomes a Caipiroska.

50ml (1¾fl oz) Cachaça – Yaguara Cachaça
15ml (½fl oz) Lime Juice
15ml (½fl oz) Sugar Syrup
½ Lime

Glassware: Rocks Glass
Ice: "Dirty"
Garnish: Lime Wedges
Preparation: Short Shake

o

Cut the half lime into four wedges. Add to a shaker with the remaining ingredients and ice, then shake and pour everything into a rocks glass, including the ice and lime. This is known as "dirty ice".

Make sure you taste before serving as limes can vary in acidity, which may throw off the balance. Add a touch of sugar syrup if necessary.

CHARLIE CHAPLIN

Created at the Waldorf Astoria Bar in New York during the early 1900s, this is a lovely fruity bitter-sweet cocktail and makes a simple and very approachable drink. Make sure you use a high-quality sloe gin and apricot brandy to ensure you get the very best flavour.

30ml (1fl oz) Sloe Gin – Plymouth Sloe Gin
30ml (1fl oz) Lime Juice
30ml (1fl oz) Apricot Brandy – Merlet L'une d'Abricot Brandy

Glassware: Coupette
Ice: Served Without
Garnish: Served Without
Preparation: Long Shake

o

Add all the ingredients to a shaker with ice and shake.
Strain into a chilled coupette and serve.

CHICAGO FIZZ

The Chicago Fizz was very popular in its day and, though originating in the Windy City, its fame spread and it was served at the Waldorf-Astoria for years leading up to Prohibition. Since then, it has rather fallen into obscurity but is well due a revival as the dark rum and ruby port make a very sophisticated and satisfying pairing.

Be very careful how much soda water you add as you don't want to dilute the cocktail too much. The egg white acts as a flavour stretcher so, with too much soda, you will compromise the flavour.

40ml (1⅖fl oz) Aged Rum - Diplomatico Reserva Exclusiva
20ml (¾fl oz) Lemon Juice
10ml (⅓fl oz) Sugar Syrup
20ml (¾fl oz) Egg White
15ml (½fl oz) Ruby Port - Dow's Fine Ruby Port
1 splash of Soda - Schweppes Soda

Glassware: Fizz Glass
Ice: Served Without
Garnish: Port Float
Preparation: Dry Shake, Quick Wet Shake, Top Soda and Float Port

o

Add all the ingredients, except the port and soda, to a shaker.
Dry shake and then wet shake (see page 22).
Strain into a chilled fizz glass, add a splash of soda, float port on top and serve.

CLASSIC CHAMPAGNE COCKTAIL

The first recorded version of this drink is from 1855, where it is mentioned without the cognac. The sugar cube stimulates the carbonation bead in the champagne, giving it extra effervescence and a little added sweetness too at the bottom of the glass. The Angostura Bitters add a beautiful complexity as a base note. Even without the cognac, it is a wonderful drink, but with the brandy, you have something decadent for a special occasion.

1 White Sugar Cube
5 dashes of Angostura Bitters
15ml (½fl oz) Cognac - Martell V.S.O.P
Top Champagne - Charles Heidsieck Brut Reserve

Glassware: Champagne Flute
Ice: Served Without
Garnish: Long Orange Twist
Preparation: Build

o

Take the white sugar cube and, away from the glass, dash the bitters on top of it.

Place the sugar cube in the glass, add the cognac and top with approximately 100ml (5⅗fl oz) Champagne. Garnish with an orange twist and serve.

CLOVER CLUB

This cocktail is a lovely combination of gin, lemon and raspberries, plus the dry vermouth adds a layer of complexity and the egg white contributes a delicious creamy mouthfeel. It has been around since the late 19th century and is named after a men's group of the same name who used to meet at The Bellevue Stratford Hotel in Philadelphia between approximately 1880 and 1920.

There are plenty of recipes for the Clover Club out there. For all our drinks, we use fresh fruit wherever we can and this drink certainly benefits from delicious fresh raspberries. However, do taste them first as they can be quite acidic and you may need a touch more sugar syrup to help balance this out.

35ml (1¼fl oz) Gin – Bombay Sapphire Gin
15ml (½fl oz) Dry Vermouth – Noilly Prat Original
25ml (⅘fl oz) Lemon Juice
25ml (⅘fl oz) Egg White
17.5ml (¾fl oz) Sugar Syrup
4 Raspberries

Glassware: Coupette
Ice: Served Without
Garnish: 1 Raspberry
Preparation: Dry Shake and Long Wet Shake

o

Add all the ingredients to the shaker. Dry shake, then follow with a wet shake.

Strain into a chilled coupette, garnish with a raspberry and serve.

CORPSE REVIVER NO. 1

From *The Savoy Cocktail Book*: "To be taken before 11am, or whenever steam and energy are needed." That says it all, really.

40ml (1⅖fl oz) Cognac – Hennessy V.S.O.P
10ml (⅓fl oz) Calvados – Christian Drouin Domaine Coeur de Lion Selection
25ml (⅘fl oz) Sweet Vermouth – Martini Rosso
2.5ml (4 dashes) Angostura Bitters

Glassware: Coupette
Ice: Served Without
Garnish: Orange Coin
Preparation: Long Stir

Add all the ingredients to a mixing glass with ice and stir.

Strain into a chilled coupette, garnish with an orange coin and serve.

CORPSE REVIVER NO. 2

Here's another Corpse Reviver or "pick-me-up" type of drink, a category that emerged in the mid-1800s: "Four of these taken in swift succession will unrevive the corpse again." (*The Savoy Cocktail Book*)

The original recipe called for Kina Lillet, but as this is no longer available there are various substitution options. Some recipes use Lillet Blanc, but we prefer to use Cocchi Americano as the flavour is a little closer to the original. However, we recommend that you try them both and see which one you like.

20ml (¾fl oz) Gin – No.3 London Dry Gin
20ml (¾fl oz) Lemon Juice
20ml (¾fl oz) Cocchi Americano
20ml (¾fl oz) Triple Sec – Cointreau
1.25ml (2 dashes) Absinthe – Pernod Absinthe

Glassware: Coupette
Ice: Served Without
Garnish: Discarded Lemon Coin
Preparation: Long Shake

○

Add all the ingredients to the shaker with ice and shake.

Strain into a chilled coupette, gently squeeze a lemon coin over the top and then serve.

COSMOPOLITAN

This perfect citrus-sweet concoction of vodka, orange liqueur, lime and cranberry is a true classic and a sure sign that it's party time. As with many classic drinks, there are a number of claims to its origin, even stretching back as far as the 1930s. However, the incarnation of the drink that is closest to the Cosmo we know and love today came about in 1988 when Toby Cecchini, at The Odeon in New York, combined cranberry juice with the newly available Absolut Citron and "the things that we were using at the time to make fresh Margaritas. It was kind of a no brainer." And then, in 1996, the legendary bartender Dale DeGroff perfected his own recipe at Manhattan's Rainbow Rooms, gave it his signature flamed orange zest garnish (although we prefer it without, as the burnt orange oils give off a unique aroma), and it became the drink of the decade.

40ml (1⅖fl oz) Citrus/Lemon Vodka - Absolut Citron
10ml (⅓fl oz) Triple Sec - Cointreau
15ml (½fl oz) Lime Juice
15ml (½fl oz) Sugar Syrup
25ml (⅘fl oz) Cranberry Juice

Glassware: Coupette
Ice: Served Without
Garnish: Discarded Orange Coin
Preparation: Long Shake

o

Add all the ingredients to a shaker with ice and shake.
Strain into a chilled coupette glass, gently squeeze an orange coin
over the top and then serve.

DAIQUIRI

The drink we recognise as the Daiquiri was believed to be invented in the very late 1800s when Jennings Stockton Cox, an American engineer, created it for his house guests, but of course there are many competing claims to its origin.

However it came about, the trinity of rum and sugar and lime is, as always, a winning combination. It's perhaps more common to use sugar syrup rather than granulated sugar as the latter never quite fully dissolves into the drink, but we actually prefer this as it gives incredible texture on the palate.

15ml Chef Spoon (½fl oz) Caster Sugar
30ml (1fl oz) Lime Juice
60ml (2fl oz) White Rum - Bacardi Ron Superior Heritage

Glassware: Coupette
Ice: Served Without
Garnish: Served Without
Preparation: Long Shake

o

Place the caster sugar and lime juice in a shaker and stir to dissolve the sugar.

Add the rum and shake with ice.

Strain into a chilled coupette and serve.

DARK 'N' STORMY

We first tried this at Attaboy in New York and have loved it ever since. The rum company, Gosling Brothers of Bermuda, owns the rights to the drink and claims it was invented at some point just after the First World War, in Bermuda, where Gosling's is based. They recommend you use Gosling's Black Seal rum, but it still works great with any dark rum. Mixing fresh ginger syrup and soda is a very tasty (and in our opinion, improved) way to make cocktails that call for ginger beer.

50ml (1¾fl oz) Gosling's Black Seal Rum
15ml (½fl oz) Lime Juice
25ml (⅘fl oz) Ginger Syrup
Top Soda – Schweppes Soda

Glassware: Highball
Ice: Block Ice
Garnish: Lime Wheel
Preparation: Quick Shake and Top with Soda

o

Add all the ingredients except the soda to the shaker with ice.
Shake, then pour into a highball glass over ice.

Top with soda, gently stir to mix, then garnish with a lime wheel and serve.

DELICIOUS SOUR

Delicious by name, delicious by nature.

William Schmidt gets the credit for this one as it first appeared in his book *The Flowing Bowl*, printed in 1892. His recipe calls for "apple jack, peach brandy, lime, egg white and soda" but these days it's common to use calvados, peach liqueur and lemon juice and to miss out the soda – it's beautifully sweet and refreshing.

35ml (1¼fl oz) Calvados - Christian Drouin Domaine Coeur de Lion Selection
15ml (½fl oz) Crème de Pêche - Merlet Crème de Pêche
25ml (⅘fl oz) Fresh Lemon Juice
25ml (⅘fl oz) Egg White
10ml (⅓fl oz) Sugar Syrup

Glassware: Coupette
Ice: Served Without
Garnish: Served Without
Preparation: Dry Shake and Long Wet Shake

○

Add all the ingredients to a shaker, then dry shake, followed by a wet shake (with ice).

Strain into a chilled coupette and serve.

THE VENNING BROTHERS

—

STONE FENCE

25ml ($^4/_5$fl oz) Woodford Reserve Kentucky Bourbon
10ml ($^1/_3$fl oz) Merlet Crème de Pêche
25ml ($^4/_5$fl oz) Fresh Lemon Juice
10ml ($^1/_3$fl oz) Sugar Syrup
5ml ($^1/_6$fl oz) Egg White
50ml (1¾fl oz) Soda Water
Top Breton Cider

Glassware: Fizz Glass
Ice: Served Without
Garnish: Served Without
Preparation: Short Shake, Soda and Cider Top

o

Add all the ingredients, except the soda and cider,
to a shaker with ice and shake.

Strain into a chilled fizz glass, top with soda and cider,
then serve.

EGGNOG

Eggnog derives from a Medieval British drink called a posset, which was a hot, milk-based beverage flavoured with spices. There are many different ways to serve it but this way, we think, is the best of all, as the complex aromatics of the tonka bean conjure up all the spicy wonders of the festive season. If tonka bean isn't available, nutmeg is a great substitution. You can play around with the base spirit and the spice served on top. We recommend aged spirits, for richness of flavour, alongside warming spices.

50g (1¾oz) Caster Sugar
1 Egg Yolk
1 Egg White
120ml (4fl oz) Milk
30ml (1fl oz) Heavy Cream
45ml (1½fl oz) Calvados – Christian Drouin Domaine Coeur de Lion Selection

Glassware: Rocks Glass
Ice: Served Without
Garnish: Grated Tonka Bean or Nutmeg
Preparation: Build

o

In a bowl, fold together the sugar and egg yolk. In a separate bowl, whip the egg whites into stiff peaks.

Add the milk, cream and calvados to the egg yolk mix and stir to combine.
Fold through fluffy egg whites and then pour into a rocks glass. Grate fresh tonka bean or nutmeg on top and serve.

EL DIABLO

The El Diablo is a great tequila cocktail. Its exact origins are unknown but it seems to have been born in California during the 1940s and was published in Trader Vic's 1946 *Book of Food and Drink* as a Mexican El Diablo.

40ml (1⅓fl oz) Blanco Tequila - Tapatio Blanco
15ml (½fl oz) Fresh Lime Juice
20ml (¾fl oz) Ginger Syrup
Top Soda - Schweppes Soda
10ml (⅓fl oz) Crème de Cassis - Merlet Crème de Cassis

Glassware: Highball
Ice: Block Ice
Garnish: Lime Wheel
Preparation: Quick Shake and Top with Soda. Float Crème de Cassis

o

Add all the ingredients, except the soda and Crème de Cassis,
to a shaker with ice and shake.

Strain into an ice-filled highball glass. Top with soda and gently stir to mix.
Float Crème de Cassis on top, garnish with a lime wheel and serve.

EL PRESIDENTE

This elegant rum-based cocktail is attributed to Eddie Woelke, an American who tended bar at the Jockey Club in Havana and who created it for the president, Gerardo Machado, who ruled Cuba from 1925 to 1933. Since then, the recipe has gone through countless variations but, for the modern palate, we love this version that uses sweet vermouth. The addition of orange bitters also helps to add an interesting underlying complexity which the drink really deserves.

40ml (1⅓fl oz) Aged Rum - Havana Club Selección de Maestros
15ml (½fl oz) Sweet Vermouth - Martini Rosso
10ml (⅓fl oz) Orange Curaçao - Pierre Ferrand Dry Curaçao
5ml (⅙fl oz) Grenadine
1 dash of Orange Bitters - Regans' Orange Bitter No.6

Glassware: Coupette
Ice: Served Without
Garnish: Orange Coin
Preparation: Long Stir

o

Add all the ingredients to a mixing glass with ice and stir.
Strain into a chilled coupette, garnish with an orange coin and serve.

RUSSELL DILLON

—

BRIGHT HATCHET

35ml (1¼fl oz) Olmeca Altos Reposado
30ml (1fl oz) Cocchi Storico Vermouth di Torino
20ml (¾fl oz) Pamplemousse Liqueur
3 drops of Bittercube Orange Bitters
2 drops of Rose Water

Glassware: Martini glass
Ice: Served Without
Garnish: Grapefruit Twist
Preparation: Long Stir

o

Add all the ingredients to a mixing glass with ice and stir.

Pour into a chilled martini glass and garnish
with a grapefruit twist and serve.

ESPRESSO MARTINI

Originally called a "Vodka Espresso", this drink was created in 1983 by Dick Bradsell at the Soho Brasserie in London for a guest who requested something to, and we quote, "wake her up and fuck her up." During the 1990s, it became better known as the Espresso Martini and, in our humble opinion, it is one of the best drinks to have been created in the last fifty years. It is beautifully simple and is now one of the most popular drinks around the world. Works great with rum or tequila as a base too!

35ml (1¼fl oz) Vodka - Grey Goose
15ml (½fl oz) Coffee Liqueur - Mr. Black Cold Brew Coffee Liqueur
10ml (⅓fl oz) Sugar Syrup
25ml (⅘fl oz) Fresh Espresso

Glassware: Coupette
Ice: Served Without
Garnish: Three Coffee Beans
Preparation: Long Shake

o

Add all the ingredients to a shaker with ice and shake.

Strain into a chilled coupette, garnish with three coffee beans and serve.

FISH HOUSE PUNCH

It's customary to recite the following poem when serving Fish House Punch: *There's a little place just out of town, Where, if you go to lunch, They'll make you forget your mother-in-law, With a drink called Fish House Punch.*

This comes from a famous Philadelphia fishing and social club called the "State in Schuylkill Fishing Corporation" and is one of the most famous punch recipes on record, probably dating from the 18th century.

20ml (¾fl oz) Cognac - Martell V.S.O.P
20ml (¾fl oz) Aged Rum - Havana Club Especial
10ml (⅓fl oz) Peach Liqueur - Merlet Crème de Pêche
25ml (⅘fl oz) Fresh Lemon Juice
40ml (1⅓fl oz) Chilled Water
10ml (⅓fl oz) Sugar Syrup

Glassware: Highball
Ice: Block Ice
Garnish: Lemon Slice
Preparation: Quick Shake

o

Add all the ingredients to a shaker with ice and shake.

Strain into a chilled highball glass with ice. Garnish with a lemon slice and serve.

FLIP

This was first seen in print in Jerry Thomas's *The Bar-Tender's Guide*, but the drink itself dates back to the 1600s, when a tankard of ale was stirred up with sugar, eggs and spices and then heated up using redhot irons from the fire. Since then, a Flip denotes any drink that contains a fortified wine or spirit, shaken with an egg and sweetened with sugar. You can therefore experiment with any spirit base (bourbon/scotch and rum) but we love the way that cognac sits with the other ingredients. Don't be put off by the raw egg – it simply gives the drink a deliciously creamy texture. The drink itself is not too distant from the Eggnog.

50ml (1¾fl oz) Cognac – Hennessy V.S.O.P
25ml (⅘fl oz) Heavy Cream
10ml (⅓fl oz) Sugar Syrup
1 Egg

Glassware: Coupette
Ice: Served Without
Garnish: Grated Nutmeg
Preparation: Dry Shake and Long Wet Shake

o

Add all the ingredients to a shaker and dry shake, followed by a wet shake (with ice).

Strain into a chilled coupette, dust the top with grated nutmeg and serve.

RYAN CHETIYAWARDANA

—

RUM & COKE FLOAT

50ml (1¾fl oz) Bacardi Añejo Cuatro
20ml (¾fl oz) Coca-Cola Syrup (see below)
1 Egg White

Glassware: Contoured Glass
Ice: Served Without
Garnish: Lime Twist
Preparation: Dry Shake and Long Wet Shake

○

Add all the ingredients to a shaker and dry shake, followed by a long
wet shake (with ice). Strain into a chilled contoured glass, garnish
with a lime twist and serve.

COCA-COLA SYRUP

Mix equal parts coke and caster sugar together.

FRENCH 75

The exact origins of this drink are unclear, but it dates back to the First World War and the name refers to the French 75-mm field gun. In France, it's simply known as a "Soixante-Quinze".

Try the French 75 with cognac for another version of this wonderful cocktail. The cognac adds a beautiful richness, but we enjoy this lighter version with gin.

30ml (1fl oz) Gin - Beefeater 24
15ml (½fl oz) Fresh Lemon Juice
10ml (⅓fl oz) Sugar Syrup
Top Champagne - Perrier-Jouët Grand Brut NV

Glassware: Champagne Flute
Ice: Served Without
Garnish: Long Lemon Peel
Preparation: Quick Shake, Top with Champagne

o

Add the gin, lemon and sugar syrup to a shaker with ice and shake.

Strain into a champagne flute and top up with Champagne.
Stir gently to mix, garnish with lemon peel and serve.

MIMI SCHOFIELD

—

TAMARA IN A GREEN BUGATTI

45ml (1½fl oz) Citadelle Original Gin
25ml (⅘fl oz) Fresh Lemon Juice
15ml (½fl oz) Sugar Syrup
2 dashes of Scrappy's Lavender Bitters
5 Mint Leaves
Top Ruinat Blanc de Blancs NV Champagne

Glassware: Rocks Glass
Ice: Block Ice
Garnish: Mint Sprig, Edible Flower, Dry Lavender Stalk
Preparation: Quick Shake, Top Champagne

∘

Add all the ingredients, except the Champagne, to a shaker with ice and shake.

Strain into a chilled rocks glass over ice and top with Champagne. Garnish
with a sprig of mint, an edible flower and a dry lavender stalk and serve.

GARIBALDI

This Campari-red drink pays tribute to General Giuseppe Garibaldi who, in his red jacket, contributed to the unification and creation of modern Italy. The drink fell into years of obscurity but has recently been championed by Naren Young at the Greenwich Village institution, Caffe Dante.

The key to a great Garibaldi is using freshly pressed orange juice. The dry shake helps aerate the drink without adding any dilution, and this is crucial to keeping the flavours intense. Unless you have a centrifugal juicer at hand. As a variation, substitute the Campari for rye and the fresh orange for fresh apple and serve in the same way – it also tastes magnificent.

35ml (1¼fl oz) Campari
100ml (3½fl oz) Fresh Orange Juice

Glassware: Rocks Glass
Ice: Block Ice
Garnish: Orange Slice
Preparation: Dry Shake

o

Add both ingredients to a shaker and dry shake.

Pour into a chilled rocks glass, garnish with an orange slice and serve.

GIMLET

The Gimlet is an old British sailors' drink. It was only in the late 1860s that they began to preserve limes with sugar (in a lime cordial), so for many years before this sailors preserved limes with alcohol and took it medicinally to prevent scurvy during their long voyages at sea.

There are two ways to make a Gimlet. The original calls for equal parts gin and lime cordial, the second is our preferred version below.

A cordial is essentially a combination of acid (lime), sugar (caster) and something to lengthen it, in most cases water. With this recipe, we are creating a fresh cordial "à la minute", giving a beautifully clean and fragrant cocktail.

60ml (2fl oz) Gin - Portobello Road Gin
30ml (1fl oz) Fresh Lime Juice
15ml Chef Spoon (½fl oz) Caster Sugar

Glassware: Coupette
Ice: Served Without
Garnish: Served Without
Preparation: Long Shake

o

Add the caster sugar and lime juice to a shaker with ice and stir to dissolve the sugar.
Add the gin and shake.
Strain into a chilled coupette and serve.

GIN & TONIC

The roots of a Gin & Tonic are thought to lie in India, where British army officers mixed quinine (to fight off malaria) with water, sugar and gin.

Made correctly, it's all you could ever ask from a drink and the key, we think, is to keep the gin present – a ratio of 3:1 works wonderfully. We also like to add a lemon aroma and flavour, but it's important to keep it subtle so that the gin is allowed to speak for itself. There are plenty of gins on the market today, so choose your favourite or experiment with different types.

50ml (1¾fl oz) Gin – Tanqueray Gin
150ml (5fl oz) Schweppes Tonic – Schweppes Indian Tonic Water

Glassware: Highball
Ice: Block Ice
Garnish: Lemon Slice and Discarded Lemon Coin
Preparation: Build

○

Place ice in a highball glass and then add the gin. Gently pour the tonic on top of the gin, and try popping as few bubbles in the tonic as possible.

Garnish with a lemon slice, gently squeeze a lemon coin over the top, and serve.

GIN FIZZ

This is a long, refreshing drink, perfect for a warm summer's day or evening. Its origins are unknown, but it was first seen in print in Jerry Thomas's *The Bar-Tender's Guide* of 1862.

We like to muddle granulated sugar and lemon peel together to release the oils from the lemon skin, which creates the same effect as an oleo-saccharum – essentially a mix of citrus oil and sugar. With the addition of egg white the drink becomes a silver fizz, while adding an egg yolk would be a golden fizz. There are many more variations in this eclectic family of drinks.

1 Lemon Peel to Shake
15ml Chef Spoon (½fl oz) Caster Sugar
30ml (1fl oz) Fresh Lemon Juice
60ml (2fl oz) Gin – Plymouth Gin
Top Soda – Schweppes Soda

Glassware: Fizz Glass
Ice: Served Without
Garnish: Lemon Peel
Preparation: Quick Shake and Top with Soda

o

Place the lemon peel and caster sugar in a shaker and muddle.
Add lemon juice and stir until the sugar has dissolved.

Add gin to the shaker with ice and shake.

Strain into a chilled fizz glass. Top up with soda water and gently mix.
Garnish with lemon peel and serve.

GODFATHER

This very simple drink became very popular in the 1970s, thanks to *The Godfather* novel (1969) and the movie adaptation (1972). Traditionally, it's made from two ingredients – scotch and amaretto – but we like to add a dash of Angostura bitters to add a touch of complexity. Otherwise, it is quite a sweet cocktail.

If you replace the scotch with vodka, it is called a Godmother. If you switch the scotch for cognac, it becomes a Godchild.

40ml (1⅓fl oz) Scotch - The Balvenie DoubleWood 12
20ml (¾fl oz) Amaretto - Luxardo Amaretto di Saschira
1 dash of Angostura Bitters

Glassware: Rocks Glass
Ice: Block Ice
Garnish: Served Without
Preparation: Short Stir

o

Add all the ingredients to a mixing glass with ice and stir.

Strain into an ice-filled rocks glass and serve.

DANIEL SCHOFIELD

—

PADRINO

40ml (1⅓fl oz) Woodford Reserve Rye
15ml (½fl oz) Luxardo Amaretto di Saschira
10ml (⅓fl oz) Gonzalez Byass Oloroso Sherry
10ml (⅓fl oz) Tio Pepe Fino Sherry
5ml (⅙fl oz) Merlet Lune d'Abricot
2 dashes of Peychaud's Bitters

Glassware: Rocks Glass
Ice: Block Ice
Garnish: Lemon Twist
Preparation: Quick Stir

o

Add all the ingredients to a mixing glass with ice and stir.

Pour into a rocks glass over ice and garnish with a lemon twist and serve.

GRASSHOPPER

Created in Tujagues, in The French Quarter of New Orleans, somewhere around 1920, the Grasshopper is sweet, mint-flavoured and fantastically green. Best served as an after-dinner drink.

35ml (1¼fl oz) Crème de Cacao Blanc - Briottet Crème de Cacao Blanc
30ml (1fl oz) Crème de Menthe Verte - Briottet Crème de Menthe Verte
2 Mint Leaves
25ml (⅘fl oz) Heavy Cream

Glassware: Coupette
Ice: Served Without
Garnish: 1 Mint Leaf
Preparation: Medium Shake

o

Add all the ingredients to a shaker with ice and shake.

Strain into a chilled coupette, garnish with a mint leaf and serve.

HANKY PANKY

The Hanky Panky was created at the turn of the 20th century for Sir Charles Hawtrey, a very famous actor in his day, by Ada Coleman in The American Bar at The Savoy. Essentially, it's a sweet martini, but made all the more interesting by the addition of Fernet Branca, which transforms the flavour.

30ml (1fl oz) Gin - Sipsmith London Dry Gin
30ml (1fl oz) Sweet Vermouth - Martini Rosso
5ml (⅙fl oz) Fernet Branca

Glassware: Coupette
Ice: Served Without
Garnish: Orange Coin
Preparation: Long Stir

o

Add all the ingredients to a mixing glass with ice and stir.

Strain into a chilled coupette, garnish with an orange coin and serve.

HEMINGWAY SPECIAL DAIQUIRI
(PAPA DOBLE)

This comes from El Floridita in Cuba and, legend has it, was made for Ernest Hemingway himself after he tried the bar's standard frozen daiquiri and apparently said, "That's good but I prefer it without sugar and with double rum." In keeping with him being a diabetic, the drink was therefore originally just a heavy measure of rum and a splash of lime juice. However, it's evolved over the years to include grapefruit juice and maraschino, and also a little sugar syrup to even out the sweet–sour balance.

50ml (1¾fl oz) Light Rum - Havana Club 3 Year Old
15ml (½fl oz) Fresh Lime Juice
30ml (1fl oz) Fresh Grapefruit Juice
10ml (⅓fl oz) Maraschino - Luxardo Maraschino
10ml (⅓fl oz) Sugar Syrup

Glassware: Coupette
Ice: Served Without
Garnish: Discarded Grapefruit Twist
Preparation: Long Shake

○

Add all the ingredients to a shaker with ice and shake.

Strain into a chilled coupette, gently squeeze a grapefruit twist over the top and then serve.

HOT TODDY

The history of this drink is much in dispute, with some pointing its origins toward India, while others toward Scotland. Our favourite version is that it takes its name from Edinburgh's Tod's Well, an important water source for the city in the 1800s, where the drink was popular.

You can have fun playing around with the spirit base and different sweeteners and spices. Bourbon, rum, brandy, nutmeg, cinnamon and cloves all work wonderfully.

50ml (1¾fl oz) Scotch – Monkey Shoulder Blended Malt
25ml (⅘fl oz) Fresh Lemon Juice
20ml (¾fl oz) Honey Syrup
50ml (1¾fl oz) Hot Water
1 dash of Orange Bitters – Regans' Orange Bitters No.6
1 dash of Angostura Bitters

Glassware: Toddy
Ice: Served Without
Garnish: Discarded Lemon Twist
Preparation: Build

o

Add all the ingredients to a toddy glass and mix gently. Gently squeeze a lemon twist over the top and then serve.

IRISH COFFEE

Mixing coffee and spirits has been popular in Europe from the mid-19th century, but the Irish Coffee we recognize today is widely attributed to Joe Sheridan, who created it in the 1940s at Foynes Airbase in Limerick, Ireland.

We consider this a drink that ticks all the boxes! And we garnish ours with grated tonka bean as we love the aromatics and interesting flavour, which plays beautifully with the vanilla cream.

30ml (1fl oz) Irish Whiskey - Jameson Irish Whiskey
100ml (3½fl oz) Hot Coffee
10ml (⅓fl oz) Sugar Syrup
Float Cold Vanilla Cream

Glassware: Irish Coffee
Ice: Served Without
Garnish: Grated Tonka Bean or Nutmeg
Preparation: Build

o

Add all the ingredients to an Irish Coffee glass and mix gently.

Float vanilla cream on top, dust with grated tonka bean or nutmeg and serve.

JACK ROSE

The origins of this drink are much disputed. However, the one thing we know for sure and that we can all agree on, is that it is delicious. Made from only three ingredients, its beauty lies in its clean simplicity – apple brandy sweetened with a little grenadine. We prefer to use lemon juice, but lime juice is also very tasty.

50ml (1¾fl oz) Applejack - Laird's Applejack Brandy
25ml (⅘fl oz) Fresh Lemon Juice
15ml (½fl oz) Grenadine

Glassware: Coupette
Ice: Served Without
Garnish: Served Without
Preparation: Long Shake

o

Add all the ingredients to a shaker with ice and shake.

Strain into a chilled coupette and serve.

JUNGLE BIRD

This Tiki-style cocktail was created in the late 1970s for the opening of the Kuala Lumpur Hilton's Aviary Bar, hence the name. We love the complexity created by the mix of rums, but you can simply use one type – either a nice, aged rum or a dark rum works best.

25ml (⅘fl oz) Jamaican Rum – Appleton Estate Reserve 8 Year Old
10ml (⅓fl oz) Dark Rum – Gosling's Black Seal Rum
15ml (½fl oz) Campari
15ml (½fl oz) Fresh Lime Juice
35ml (1¼fl oz) Fresh Pineapple Juice
10ml (⅓fl oz) Sugar Syrup

Glassware: Rocks Glass
Ice: Block Ice
Garnish: Pineapple Wedge and Mint Sprig
Preparation: Medium Shake

o

Add all the ingredients to a shaker with ice and shake.

Strain into an ice-filled rocks glass, garnish with a pineapple wedge and a sprig of mint and serve.

KIR ROYALE

This is a sparkling version of the iconic French Kir aperitif. The original is made with Bourgogne Aligote, a lovely white Burgundy wine that is pale gold in colour, and was apparently first mixed at the turn of the 20th century at Café George in Dijon, France. It also tastes delicious, but the Champagne in a "Royale" means that it is, nowadays, the more popular drink. It also works very well with other liqueurs such as pear or raspberry.

10ml (⅓fl oz) Crème de Cassis - Merlet Crème de Cassis
100ml (3½fl oz) Champagne - Pol Roger Brut Réserve NV

Glassware: Champagne Flute
Ice: Served Without
Garnish: Served Without
Preparation: Build

○

Add both ingredients to a champagne flute, gently stir to mix and serve.

LAST WORD

Created by Frank Fogarty around 1920 at the Detroit Athletic Club in, you guessed it, Detroit, this is a gin-based Prohibition-era cocktail made up of equal parts gin, green Chartreuse, maraschino liqueur and lime juice. It is fresh, herbal and packs a punch.

25ml (⅘fl oz) Gin - Tanqueray No. Ten Gin
25ml (⅘fl oz) Chartreuse Green
25ml (⅘fl oz) Maraschino - Luxardo Maraschino
25ml (⅘fl oz) Lime Juice

Glassware: Coupette
Ice: Served Without
Garnish: Cherry
Preparation: Long Shake

o

Add all the ingredients to a shaker with ice and shake.
Strain into a chilled coupette, garnish with a cherry and serve.

Tip: Make sure you wash your cherries before you garnish. They often come preserved in a sweet syrup and this will unbalance the drink if you're not careful.

LAUREN MOTE

—

CHARTREUSE MILKSHAKE

45ml (1½fl oz) Tanqueray No. Ten
15ml (½fl oz) White Crème de Cacao
15ml (½fl oz) Chartreuse Green
15ml (½fl oz) Fresh Orange Juice
15ml (½fl oz) Fresh Lime Juice
20ml Sugar Syrup (see page 32)
1 Egg White
2 Dashes of Bittered Sling Malagasy Chocolate Bitters

Glassware: Highball
Ice: Block Ice
Garnish: Crushed Raw Cacao Bean
Preparation: Medium Shake

o

Add all the ingredients to a shaker with ice and shake.

Strain into a chilled highball glass, garnish with a crushed raw
cacao bean and serve.

LONG ISLAND ICED TEA

Robert Butt lays claim to the invention of this drink in 1972, while he was working at the Oak Beach Inn, Babylon, New York, an area of the state known as Long Island. It's a drink that isn't always positively associated with the disco era but, if you get the balance right, it can be quite pleasant. The trick is to have it resemble a glass of iced tea, so don't be too heavy-handed with the coke – just a splash should do.

10ml (⅓fl oz) Vodka - Reyka
10ml (⅓fl oz) Gin - Bombay Sapphire Gin
10ml (⅓fl oz) Rum - Havana 3 Club 3 Year Old Rum
10ml (⅓fl oz) Tequila - Tapatio Blanco
10ml (⅓fl oz) Triple Sec - Cointreau
25ml (⅘fl oz) Fresh Lemon Juice
10ml (⅓fl oz) Sugar Syrup
Top Coca-Cola

Glassware: Highball
Ice: Block Ice
Garnish: Lemon Slice
Preparation: Quick Shake and Top with Coca-Cola

o

Add all the ingredients, except the Coca-Cola, to a shaker with ice and shake.

Strain into an ice-filled highball glass and top with Coca-Cola.

Gently stir to mix, garnish with a lemon slice and serve.

MAI TAI

This was created in 1944 by Victor Jules Bergeron, aka Trader Vic. He made it for his friends, Ham and Carrie Guild, and, after the first sip, Carrie purportedly said "Mai tai-roa ae" which, in Tahitain, means "Out of this world, the best."

We like to use two different rums as the blend creates a lovely complex flavour, similar in profile, apparently, to the original rum used all those years ago. Wray & Nephew 17 soared in popularity with this drink and quickly became unavailable. However, the drink also works well with any type of aged rum, if the blend isn't at hand.

25ml (⅘fl oz) Jamaican Rum – Appleton Estate Reserve 8 Year Old Rum
25ml (⅘fl oz) Aged Agricole Rum – Trois Rivières VSOP
30ml (1fl oz) Lime Juice
10ml (⅓fl oz) Orange Curaçao – Pierre Ferrand Dry Curaçao
10ml (⅓fl oz) Orgeat – Small Hands Orgeat
1 dash of Angostura Bitters

Glassware: Rocks Glass
Ice: Block Ice
Garnish: Lime Wheel and Mint Sprig
Preparation: Medium Shake

○

Add all the ingredients to a shaker with ice and shake.

Strain into an ice-filled rocks glass, garnish with a lime wheel and a sprig of mint and serve.

MANHATTAN

The origins of this drink are not at all clear, but it is assumed that it is from New York in the latter half of the 19th century. These days, it is perfectly acceptable to make it with bourbon or rye, although purists will always use rye.

To make a "Perfect Manhattan", use 12.5ml dry vermouth and 12.5ml sweet vermouth, and garnish with an orange coin. To make it a "Dry Manhattan", use 25ml dry vermouth and garnish with a lemon coin. We prefer those specific garnishes for those versions of the Manhattan, but in our humble opinion, it should almost always be made "Sweet", as it is here.

50ml (1¾fl oz) Rye - Woodford Reserve Rye
25ml (⅘fl oz) Sweet Vermouth - Asterley Bros. Estate English Vermouth
2.5ml (4 dashes) Angostura Bitters

Glassware: Coupette
Ice: Served Without
Garnish: Cherry
Preparation: Long Stir

o

Add all the ingredients to a mixing glass with ice and stir.
Strain into a chilled coupette, garnish with a cherry and serve.

ALEX KRATENA

—

OYE MI CANTO

30ml (1fl oz) Tamarind-infused Blanco Tequila (see below)
60ml (2fl oz) Martini Rosato Vermouth
5ml (⅙fl oz) Del Maguey Chichichapa
1 dash of Mandarin Bitters

Glassware: Coupette
Ice: Block Ice
Garnish: Apple Blossom and Jasmine Flowers
Preparation: Long Stir

○

Add all ingredients to a mixing glass with ice and stir.
Pour into a coupette glass over ice, garnish and serve.

TAMARIND-INFUSED BLANCO TEQUILA

350g (12½oz) Tamarind
1 litre (35fl oz) Blanco Tequila

Cut the tamarind into small pieces and place with the blanco tequila in
a vacuum-sealed bag. Infuse for 48 hours, then strain using a superbag.

MARGARITA

Margarita is the Spanish word for "daisy" and this was the name of a very popular drink during the first half of the 20th century, which also consisted of a spirit, citrus and a liqueur. However, there is also a cocktail called a Picador, which is included in the Café Royale Cocktail Book of 1939, and essentially it is a Margarita with no salt rim, so many see this as the drink's first incarnation.

There are many ways to serve a Margarita – straight up, on the rocks or frozen are some of the most common calls, while whether to include a salt rim is down to personal preference too.

If you omit the sugar syrup and a salt rim and replace the Cointreau for Crème d'Apricot, it becomes a Toreador.

50ml (1¾fl oz) Blanco Tequila – Herradura Plata Blanco
25ml (⅘fl oz) Fresh Lime Juice
25ml (⅘fl oz) Triple Sec – Cointreau
5ml (⅙fl oz) Sugar Syrup

Glassware: Coupette
Ice: Served Without
Garnish: Salt Rim
Preparation: Long Shake

○

First prepare the glass with a salt rim (see page 31).
Add all the ingredients to a shaker with ice and shake.
Strain into the salt-rimmed glass and serve.

MARTINEZ

In cocktail history, the Martinez arrives around the 1860s, a little time after the Manhattan and before the Martini and first appears in print in O. H. Byron's *The Modern Bartender* of 1884.

There have been many many recipes for a Martinez over the years as almost every bartender has their own way of making it, but this is the version we like. The different layers of ingredients create a beautiful complexity and, in our opinion, the sweet vermouth makes a much more delicious cocktail than its dry vermouth counterpart.

40ml (1⅓fl oz) Gin - Fords Gin
20ml (¾fl oz) Sweet Vermouth - Cocchi Storico Vermouth di Torino
2.5ml (4 dashes) Maraschino - Luxardo Maraschino
1.25ml (2 dashes) Orange Bitters - Regans' Orange Bitters No.6
1.25ml (2 dashes) Angostura Bitters

Glassware: Coupette
Ice: Served Without
Garnish: Orange Coin
Preparation: Long Stir

o

Add all the ingredients to a mixing glass with ice and stir.
Strain into a chilled coupette, garnish with an orange coin and serve.

EZRA STAR

—

1910

20ml (¾fl oz) Del Maguey Mezcal Vida
20ml (¾fl oz) Pierre Ferrand Ambre
15ml (½fl oz) Luxardo Maraschino
30ml (1fl oz) Punt E Mes
2 dashes of Peychaud's Bitters

Glassware: Coupette
Ice: Served Without
Garnish: Orange Coin
Preparation: Long Stir

○

Add all the ingredients to a mixing glass with ice and stir.

Pour into a chilled coupette, garnish with an orange coin and serve.

MARTINI

The Martini is a diehard classic (it hardly needs to be said) and proves how the key to perfection is almost always simplicity – gin and dry vermouth. It's unclear quite who is to credit for its invention, but wiser men than us say that it evolved from the Manhattan by way of the Martinez and somewhere in the United States. H. L. Mencken called it "The only American invention as perfect as the sonnet."

A Martini is a very personal thing, and everyone has their preference – dry, wet, dirty, shaken, stirred. Below is our house style, but for a Dry Martini, we use 60ml (2fl oz) gin and 5ml (⅙fl oz) dry vermouth, for a Wet Martini a little more vermouth (15ml or ½fl oz). If made with Vodka, it is less commonly known as a Kangaroo, but for us a Martini should always be gin. For a Dirty version, use bright green Nocellera olives from Sicily, which are mild and buttery. Muddle three with 60ml (2fl oz) Vodka and 5ml (⅙fl oz) dry vermouth.

60ml (2fl oz) Gin - Tanqueray Gin
10ml (⅓fl oz) Dry Vermouth - Noilly Prat Original
1 drop of Orange Bitters - Regans' Orange Bitters No.6

Glassware: Martini Glass
Ice: Served Without
Garnish: Green Sicilian Olive or Lemon Coin
Preparation: Long Stir

○

Add all the ingredients to a mixing glass with ice and stir.

Strain into a chilled martini glass. Garnish with a lemon coin or a green olive, according to your preference, and serve.

MILANO TORINO

The Milano Torino (often shortened to "Mi-To") is a stunningly simple but delicious aperitif, created at some point during the 1860s by Gaspare Campari at the Caffè Campari in Milan. It's an equal-parts, perfectly balanced partnership of bitter and sweet, which works so well that it led to the creation of two further cocktail classics; the Americano (see page 48) and the Negroni (see page 154).

50ml (1¾fl oz) Campari
50ml (1¾fl oz) Sweet Vermouth – Cocchi Storico Vermouth di Torino

Glassware: Rocks Glass
Ice: Block Ice
Garnish: Orange Slice and Discarded Orange Coin
Preparation: Build

o

Add both ingredients to a rocks glass with ice and stir to mix, dilute slightly and chill.

Garnish with an orange slice, gently squeeze a orange coin over the top and then serve.

MINT JULEP

A Mint Julep is a lovely and refreshing whisky cocktail that has had associations with the American South since the 18th century, and is now "the drink of the Kentucky Derby", where people drink almost nothing else! However, the Julep is thought to have origins in Persia, where a "gulab" was a drink made with sweetened rose water.

The whisky and mint pairing here works so well that, if you have the time, it's worth mixing the ingredients without ice and allowing them to infuse for some time. You can also place the mint sprigs next to the straw to emphasize the aroma.

50ml (1¾fl oz) Bourbon - Four Roses Single Barrel Bourbon
10ml (⅓fl oz) Sugar Syrup
8–10 Mint Leaves

Glassware: Julep Tin or Rocks Glass
Ice: Crushed
Garnish: Mint Sprig
Preparation: Build and Churn

o

Place all the ingredients in a julep tin. Add crushed ice and churn to mix.

Top with a little more crushed ice and an abundance of mint sprigs next to the straw and serve.

MOJITO

The first reference to a drink that resembles a Mojito was made in the 16th century to an "El Draque", a concoction of aguardiente de cana (trans. *burning water* and basically a crude form of rum), lime, sugar and mint. According to legend, it was created in response to an outbreak of dysentery and scurvy on the ship of Sir Frances Drake – hence the name – and the medicine was acquired when a small boarding party went ashore on Cuba. Whatever the origin, it's a uniquely refreshing drink and almost synonymous with summer.

Adding the mint before the sugar syrup helps to extract the flavour. It's also best to build the drink quickly and to serve it straight away so you retain the flavours before too much dilution takes place. Finally, make sure the lime juice is freshly squeezed.

50ml (1¾fl oz) White Rum - Plantation 3 Stars
25ml (⅘fl oz) Fresh Lime Juice
8–10 Mint Leaves
20ml (¾fl oz) Sugar Syrup
Top Soda - Schweppes Soda

Glassware: Highball
Ice: Crushed
Garnish: Mint Sprig
Preparation: Build and Churn and Top Soda

o

Add all the ingredients, except the soda, to a highball glass and add crushed ice.

Top with soda and gently churn to make sure all the ingredients are mixed.
Garnish with a sprig of mint and serve.

MORNING GLORY FIZZ

First mentioned in George Winter's *How to Mix Drinks*, from 1884, this old-fashioned classic hails from a time when it was customary, after a hard night's drinking, to head to the bar again the following morning for a much-needed pick-me-up. However, its deliciously sour and aromatic flavours, as well as the beautiful texture provided by the egg white, make it a drink that's suitable for any occasion and its growing popularity these days is well-deserved.

50ml (1¾fl oz) Scotch – Dewar's 12 Year Old
25ml (⅘fl oz) Fresh Lemon Juice
15ml (½fl oz) Sugar Syrup
25ml (⅘fl oz) Egg White
2.5ml (4 dashes) Absinthe – Pernod Absinthe
Top Soda – Schweppes Soda

Glassware: Fizz Glass
Ice: Served Without
Garnish: Served Without
Preparation: Dry Shake, Quick Wet Shake, Top Soda

o

Place all the ingredients, except the soda, in a shaker and dry shake,
followed by a wet shake (with ice).
Strain into a chilled fizz glass, top with soda and serve.

MOSCOW MULE

Legend has it that the Moscow Mule was born when John Martin (with the rights to Smirnoff Vodka) and Jack Morgan (with his own Ginger Beer label) had a drink together at New York's Chatham Bar in 1939 and, ever savvy, they served it in a copper mug as these were produced in a factory owned by Jack Morgan's business partner at the time.

However, the more likely story is that it was put together at the Cock 'n' Bull saloon in Los Angeles and owes its origins to a stock clearance of the restaurant's basement. Either way, no-one can deny that vodka and ginger beer make a fine pairing, and it's deliciously simple to make.

You can also experiment with changing the spirit base – try it with gin, bourbon or even tequila for interesting variations.

50ml (1¾fl oz) Vodka - Belvedere
15ml (½fl oz) Fresh Lime Juice
25ml (⅘fl oz) Ginger Syrup
Top Soda - Schweppes Soda

Glassware: Highball
Ice: Block Ice
Garnish: Lime Wheel and 3 Dashes Angostura Bitters
Preparation: Quick Shake and Top Soda

o

Add all the ingredients, except the soda, to a shaker with ice and shake.

Pour into a highball glass over ice. Top with soda and gently stir to mix.
Garnish with a lime wheel and serve.

MULATA DAIQUIRI

This richly aromatic and smooth cocktail is essentially a classic Daiquiri (see page 91) made with aged rum and a hint of chocolate. For a variation, try it with white rum and crème de cacao blanc as the vanilla notes from the white chocolate add a lovely rich creaminess.

40ml (1⅓fl oz) Aged Rum - Bacardi 8 Year Old Rum
25ml (⅘fl oz) Fresh Lime Juice
10ml (⅓fl oz) Crème de Cacao - Bols Crème de Cacao Brown
10ml (⅓fl oz) Sugar Syrup

Glassware: Coupette
Ice: Served Without
Garnish: Served Without
Preparation: Long Shake

o

Add all the ingredients to a shaker with ice and shake.

Strain into a chilled coupette and serve.

AGO PERRONE

—

MULATA DAISY

45ml (1½fl oz) Bacardi Carta Blanca
20ml (¾fl oz) Fresh Lime Juice
15ml (½fl oz) Dark Crème de Cacao
10ml (⅓fl oz) Galliano L'Autentico
1 Bar Spoon (5ml or ⅙fl oz) Granulated Sugar
1 Bar Spoon (5ml or ⅙fl oz) Fennel Seeds

Glassware: Coupette
Ice: Served Without
Garnish: Cacao Powder Rim
Preparation: Long Shake

o

First prepare the coupette with a cacao powder rim as you would a sugar rim.

Add all the ingredients to a shaker with ice and shake.

Strain into the glass and serve.

NEGRONI

Legend has it that, in 1919, the Italian count, Camillo Negroni, walked into the Casoni Bar in Florence, needing something a little stronger than his traditional Americano (see page 48). His friend and bartender, Fosco Scarselli, substituted gin for soda and the Negroni was born.

The secret to a great Negroni is in not over-diluting it, so a quick stir is more than enough during preparation. Also, as it's a drink that can sit on ice for some time, it's even better if you can work with ingredients that are already chilled and to pour over ice.

25ml (⅘fl oz) Gin - Tanqueray Gin
25ml (⅘fl oz) Campari
25ml (⅘fl oz) Sweet Vermouth - Asterley Bros. Estate English Vermouth

Glassware: Rocks Glass
Ice: Block Ice
Garnish: Orange Slice and Discarded Orange Coin
Preparation: Build

o

Add all the ingredients to an ice-filled rocks glass and stir quickly.

Garnish with an orange slice, gently squeeze an orange coin
over the top and then serve.

JAKE BURGER

—

THE QUEEN MOTHER COCKTAIL

25ml (⅘fl oz) Portobello Road Gin
25ml (⅘fl oz) Dubonnet
20ml (¾fl oz) Aperol
5ml (⅙fl oz) Myers's Jamaican Rum

Glassware: Martini Glass
Ice: Served Without
Garnish: Orange and Lemon Coins
Preparation: Long Stir

o

Add all the ingredients to a mixing glass with ice and stir.
Pour into a chilled martini glass, garnish with an orange
and lemon coin and serve.

NEW YORK SOUR

This one is from the late 1800s, where it was known under a plethora of names (Continental Sour, Southern Whiskey Sour, Brunswick Sour, Claret Snap) before finally it settled on the New York Sour. Essentially, it's a whisky sour with a red wine float, which visually looks beautiful and adds an extra depth of flavour.

Most recipes call for the drink to be served in a rocks glass, but we think all sours taste better in a coupette as it prevents too much dilution. For the red wine, we recommend something full-bodied, like a Malbec or a Shiraz.

50ml (1¾fl oz) Bourbon – Bulleit Bourbon Whiskey
25ml (⅘fl oz) Fresh Lemon Juice
15ml (½fl oz) Sugar Syrup
25ml (⅘fl oz) Egg White
20ml (¾fl oz) Red Wine Float

Glassware: Coupette
Ice: Served Without
Garnish: Red Wine Float
Preparation: Dry Shake, Quick Wet Shake and Float

○

Add all the ingredients, except the red wine, to a shaker.
Dry shake and then wet shake (with ice).
Strain into a chilled coupette, float the red wine on top and serve.

OLD FASHIONED

In the late 19th century, the American cocktail scene was awash with new drinks made with all manner of spirits, bitters, fruit juices and syrups, and of course it wasn't to everybody's tastes. There were the old timers who wanted none of the new-fangled nonsense, just a simple cocktail, as it was defined in 1806 as made up of a spirit, sugar, water and bitters. Therefore, we like to think of all the people all over the United States, asking for a cocktail the "old-fashioned way", who can we thank for this invention? Perhaps the Pendennis Club in Louisville, who lay claim, but who is to know.

In our opinion, an Old Fashioned should be made quickly. We've substituted sugar syrup for the sugar cube and soda water as this can be used in a much more controlled fashion, which we prefer. You can also substitute rye for bourbon, scotch or even cognac – they all work really well.

50ml (1¾fl oz) Bourbon – Woodford Reserve Bourbon
7.5ml (¼fl oz) Sugar Syrup
2.5ml (4 dashes) Angostura Bitters

Glassware: Rocks Glass
Ice: Block Ice
Garnish: Orange Twist
Preparation: Medium Stir

o

Add all the ingredients to a mixing glass with ice and stir.

Pour into a rocks glass over ice, garnish with an orange twist and serve.

DECLAN MCGURK

—

BOURBON AND BUTTER

50ml (1¾fl oz) Michter's US*1 Kentucky Straight Bourbon
10ml (⅓fl oz) Cacao Liqueur
10ml (⅓fl oz) Orgeat Syrup
1 Bar Spoon (5ml or ⅙fl oz) Smooth Peanut Butter

Glassware: Coupette
Ice: Served Without
Garnish: A Smile
Preparation: Long Shake

○

Add all the ingredients to a shaker with ice and shake.

Strain into a chilled coupette and serve.

PALOMA

Paloma means "dove" in Spanish. It's a refreshing, long, tequila-based cocktail and was created by Don Javier Delgado Corona from La Capilla (The Chapel) in Tequila, Mexico.

For the freshest, fruitiest flavour, try to find a high-quality grapefruit soda, such as Three Cents.

50ml (1¾fl oz) Blanco Tequila - Ocho Blanco
15ml (½fl oz) Fresh Lime Juice
Top Pink Grapefruit Soda - Three Cents

Glassware: Highball
Ice: Block Ice
Garnish: Salt Rim
Preparation: Build

○

First prepare the highball glass with a salt rim (see page 31).
Add all the ingredients to the glass with ice, gently stir to mix then serve.

PEGU CLUB

This citrussy gin-based concoction comes from Burma, where it was the signature drink of a gentlemen's club called The Pegu Club in the 1920s.

A complex and originally dry and citrus lead cocktail. We find these proportions work best, especially with the addition of a touch of sugar syrup.

40ml (1⅓fl oz) Gin – Gin Mare
25ml (⅘fl oz) Fresh Lime Juice
10ml (⅓fl oz) Orange Curaçao – Pierre Ferrand Dry Curaçao
10ml (⅓fl oz) Sugar Syrup
1 dash of Orange Bitters – Regans' Orange Bitters No. 6
1 dash of Angostura Bitters

Glassware: Coupette
Ice: Served Without
Garnish: Lime Wedge
Preparation: Long Shake

○

Add all the ingredients to a shaker with ice and shake.
Strain into a chilled coupette, garnish with a lime wedge and serve.

PENDENNIS CLUB

This pretty, pink, gin-based cocktail is closely related to the Pegu Club, but comes from the Pendennis Club in Louisville Kentucky and uses apricot brandy instead of curaçao and Peychaud's bitters, which add an interesting and bright flavour profile. Again, the additional touch of sugar syrup helps create a beautiful balance of sweet, floral and fruit flavours.

40ml (1⅓fl oz) Gin – Old Young's 1829 Gin
25ml (⅘fl oz) Lime Juice
10ml (⅓fl oz) Apricot Brandy – Merlet L'une d'Abricot Brandy
10ml (⅓fl oz) Sugar Syrup
2.5ml (4 dashes) Peychaud's Bitters

Glassware: Coupette
Ice: Served Without
Garnish: Lime Wedge
Preparation: Long Shake

o

Add all the ingredients to a shaker with ice and shake.
Strain into a chilled coupette, garnish with a lime wedge and serve.

PENICILLIN

Created by Sam Ross in 2005 at Milk & Honey, New York, this originated as a riff on one of the bar's bestselling cocktails, the Gold Rush. It takes the latter (bourbon, lemon juice and honey syrup) and adds a spicy note of ginger and a smoky layer of Islay Whisky to make a drink that conjures up the medicinal qualities of a Hot Toddy and is always precisely what the doctor ordered.

This recipe is kindly provided by its creator, Sam Ross.

55ml (1⅘fl oz) Scotch – Dewar's 12 Year Old
20ml (¾fl oz) Fresh Lemon Juice
10ml (⅓fl oz) Honey Syrup
10ml (⅓fl oz) Ginger Syrup
7.5ml (¼fl oz) Islay Whisky – Lagavulin 16 Year Old

Glassware: Rocks Glass
Ice: Block Ice
Garnish: Candied Ginger
Preparation: Medium Shake and Whisky Float

o

Add all the ingredients, except the Islay whisky, to a shaker with ice and shake.

Strain into a chilled ice-filled rocks glass, float the Islay whisky on top,
garnish with candied ginger and serve.

PIMMS CUP

Pimms No.1, a slightly spicy and citrussy gin-based liqueur, was created in 1823. It is unclear when it began to be served as it is today with chopped garnishes of fruit, cucumber and herbs – who cares, really – it is an English summer's day in a glass. Equally pleasing with lemonade as it is with ginger ale, we slightly prefer the latter and find that a touch of fresh lime juice helps counterbalance the sweetness of the liqueur.

50ml (1¾fl oz) PIMMS No.1
10ml (⅓fl oz) Fresh Lime Juice
1 Strawberry
4–6 Mint Leaves
3 Slices of Cucumber
1 Slice of Orange
Top Ginger Ale – Schweppes Ginger Ale

Glassware: Highball
Ice: Block Ice
Garnish: Mint Sprig
Preparation: Build

o

Add all the ingredients, except the ginger ale, to a highball glass and muddle.

Add ice, top with ginger ale and stir gently to mix.

Garnish with a sprig of mint and serve.

PIÑA COLADA

Three bartenders claim this famous cocktail as their own: Ramón "Monchito" Marrero Pérez says he made the first Piña Colada at the Caribe Hilton's Beachcomber Bar in 1952, while his colleague there, Ricardo Garcia, contests it as his own invention, and then there's also Don Ramón Portas Mingot, who says he created it at a Puerto Rican restaurant, the Barrachina, in 1963.

The drink is not mentioned in cocktail books until the late 1960s, so we'll probably never know the full story. What everyone can agree on is that the trinity of rum, pineapple and coconut is a winning combination and, in our opinion, a touch of lime and a dash of Angostura bitters rounds off this drink beautifully. Use the best-quality pineapple juice, and avoid adding too much crushed ice as it will dilute the drink.

50ml (1¾fl oz) Golden Rum – Havana Club Especial
60ml (2fl oz) Fresh Pineapple Juice
30ml (1fl oz) Coco Lopez Cream of Coconut
1 dash of Angostura Bitters
5ml (⅙fl oz) Fresh Lime Juice
Pinch of Salt

Glassware: Highball
Ice: Served Without
Garnish: Pineapple Wedge
Preparation: Blend

o

Blend all the ingredients with a little crushed ice.
Pour into a highball glass, garnish with a pineapple wedge and serve.

CHRIS MOORE

—

CHAMPAGNE PIÑA COLADA

20ml (¾fl oz) Bacardi Ron Superior Heritage
5ml (⅙fl oz) Trois Rivières Blanc Agricole
40ml (1⅓fl oz) Fresh Pineapple Juice
35ml (1¼fl oz) Pineapple Cordial (see below)
2 scoops Coconut Sorbet
35ml (1¼fl oz) Möet & Chandon Brut Champagne

Glassware: Highball
Ice: Served Without
Garnish: Dried Coconut Chips
Preparation: Blend

o

Add all the ingredients, except the Champagne, to a blender with ice and
blend until smooth. Add the Champagne to a highball glass, then pour
the blended mixture on top. Garnish with dried coconut chips and serve.

PINEAPPLE CORDIAL

500g Fresh Pineapple Juice
250g Caster Sugar
5g Citric Acid

Stir to combine all the ingredients.

PINK GIN

Like a Gin & Tonic, Pink Gin came about as a medical cure and its origins go back to the 19th century, when sailors in The Royal Navy were given Angostura bitters as an antidote for seasickness. These bitters tasted rather revolting on their own and yet became a lot more palatable when taken along with a stiff gin. The bitters turned the gin pink and a rather delicious cocktail was born.

Historically, this drink should be served slightly warm and without any dilution as of course there was no ice at sea. We rather like it served cold and diluted (although you can use gin that has been chilled in the freezer), but we prefer the drink with the addition of Peychaud's bitters and a little sweetness to round off the edges.

60ml (2fl oz) Gin - Plymouth Gin
1 dash of Angostura Bitters
3 dashes of Peychaud's Bitters
5ml (⅙fl oz) Sugar Syrup

Glassware: Coupette
Ice: Served Without
Garnish: Lemon Coin
Preparation: Long Stir

o

Add all the ingredients to a mixing glass with ice and stir.
Strain into a chilled coupette, garnish with a lemon coin and serve.

PINK LADY

This classic cocktail was named after the Broadway musical of 1911 and its creator is unknown. It's a lovely variation on the fruity–sour theme and makes a very smooth drink, with nuanced complexity.

25ml (⅘fl oz) Gin - Beefeater London Dry
25ml (⅘fl oz) Applejack - Laird's Applejack Brandy
25ml (⅘fl oz) Fresh Lemon Juice
25ml (⅘fl oz) Egg White
15ml (½fl oz) Grenadine

Glassware: Coupette
Ice: Served Without
Garnish: Served Without
Preparation: Dry Shake and Long Wet Shake

o

Add all the ingredients to a shaker and dry shake, followed by a wet shake (with ice).
Strain into a chilled coupette and serve.

PISCO SOUR

This is a stunning sour and one of our favourites. Its origins are much disputed, and Chile and Peru both like to think of it as their own. However, its legendary greatness has much to do with an American called Victor Morris, who emigrated from Salt Lake City to Peru and who, one night, as the story goes, ran out of stock while making Whisky Sours and turned to the local spirit, Pisco, instead. In 1916, he opened his own establishment, which became famous for Pisco Sours and its popularity spread.

It can be made with lemon or lime juice, or a mix of both. Some people also like to blend it, but we think it's best shaken and served straight up. A final stripe of Angostura bitters then provides a wonderful aroma.

50ml (1¾fl oz) Pisco - La Caravedo
25ml (⅘fl oz) Fresh Lemon Juice
15ml (½fl oz) Sugar Syrup
25ml (⅘fl oz) Egg White

Glassware: Coupette
Ice: Served Without
Garnish: Angostura Bitters Stripe
Preparation: Dry Shake and Long Wet Shake

o

Add all the ingredients to a shaker and dry shake, followed by a wet shake (with ice).
Strain into a chilled coupette, garnish with a bitters stripe and serve.

PLANTER'S PUNCH

This is a lovely complex punch cocktail. Once again, its origins are disputed, and while some say it comes from the Planters Hotel in Charleston, South Carolina, others say a Jamaican planter's wife created it to cool down the workers. There are also many different ways to spin this mix of rum, lime, sugar and water, but we love this formula.

50ml (1¾fl oz) Myers's Rum
25ml (⅘fl oz) Lime Juice
15ml (½fl oz) Sugar Syrup
2.5ml (4 dashes) Angostura Bitters
Top Soda – Schweppes Soda

Glassware: Highball
Ice: Block Ice
Garnish: Lime Wheel
Preparation: Quick Shake and Top Soda

o

Add all the ingredients, except the soda, to a shaker with ice and shake.

Pour into an ice-filled highball glass and top with soda. Gently stir to mix,
garnish with a lime wheel and serve.

RAMOS GIN FIZZ

This is an incredible drink – the perfect balance of sweet and sour, and with a beautifully light creamy texture. It was invented in 1888 by Henry Charles Ramos at The Imperial Cabinet Saloon in New Orleans, and the traditional method requires you to shake "until you can't hear the ice". However, this is time-consuming and exhausting and, in fact, there is no need. The trick is to pour the shaken cocktail and soda into the glass at the same time, in one continuous stream, to the top, as this technique creates a beautiful "head" and exactly the right texture. Wait a few moments and top the cocktail up again. Don't substitute light for heavy cream as the latter is essential – a good Ramos is one where your straw can stand up on its own in the middle of the glass.

60ml (2fl oz) Gin - Fords Gin
15ml (½fl oz) Fresh Lemon Juice
15ml (½fl oz) Fresh Lime Juice
25ml (⅘fl oz) Sugar Syrup
25ml (⅘fl oz) Heavy Cream
25ml (⅘fl oz) Egg White
2.5ml (4 dashes) Orange Flower Water
Top Soda - Schweppes Soda

Glassware: Fizz Glass
Ice: Served Without
Garnish: Served Without
Preparation: Dry Shake, Long Wet Shake, Top Soda

o

Place all the ingredients, except the soda, in a shaker and dry shake, then wet shake (with ice). Strain into a chilled fizz glass while, at the same time, pouring in the soda.

RICKEY

This is a long, refreshing gin cocktail and is attributed to George A. Williamson who apparently, in 1880, witnessed Colonel Joe Rickey squeeze a lime into his whisky before topping up with soda and therefore named the drink after him.

It provides a great formula to play around with. We love to add liqueurs, such as rhubarb or grapefruit, but it's important to cut back on the sugar syrup if you do this, so as to balance out the sweetness. We think the best version of this is with a great and aromatic gin.

50ml (1¾fl oz) Gin – Hendrick's Gin
20ml (¾fl oz) Fresh Lime Juice
12.5ml (⅖fl oz) Sugar Syrup
Top Soda – Schweppes Soda

Glassware: Highball
Ice: Block Ice
Garnish: Lime Wheel
Preparation: Quick Shake and Top Soda

○

Add all the ingredients, except the soda, to a shaker with ice and shake.

Strain into a highball glass over ice and top with soda. Stir gently to mix, garnish with a lime wheel and serve.

ROB ROY

This was created in 1894 at the Waldorf Astoria in New York and was named after the musical (about the Scottish outlaw, Rob Roy) that was playing on Broadway at the time. Essentially, it's a scotch Manhattan. We think it works best with a balanced scotch, but it's also lovely with a single malt – an Islay whisky works wonders here! The peat from the Islay whisky is a great contrast to the sweetness from the vermouth.

50ml (1¾fl oz) Scotch – The Macallan 12 Year Old Double Cask
25ml (⅘fl oz) Sweet Vermouth – Cocchi Storico Vermouth di Torino
2.5ml (4 dashes) Angostura Bitters

Glassware: Coupette
Ice: Served Without
Garnish: Cherry
Preparation: Long Stir

o

Add all the ingredients to a mixing glass with ice and stir.
Pour into a chilled coupette, garnish with a cherry and serve.

RUM OLD FASHIONED

This is a lovely riff on the Old Fashioned classic (see page 158). However, it calls for less sugar than its Bourbon-based brother as otherwise the sweetness of the rum unbalances the drink. If you make it with a demerara rum from Guyana, it is sensational.

50ml (1¾fl oz) Aged Rum – El Dorado 12 Year Old Rum
5ml (⅙fl oz) Sugar Syrup
2.5ml (4 dashes) Angostura Bitters

Glassware: Rocks Glass
Ice: Block Ice
Garnish: Orange Twist
Preparation: Medium Stir

○

Add all the ingredients to a mixing glass with ice and stir.

Pour into a rocks glass over ice, garnish with an orange twist and serve.

RUSSIAN SPRING PUNCH

This stunning red punch is another Dick Bradsell creation from the 1980s and is, in his own words, "a sledgehammer of a drink". This refers to the fact that it conforms to the classic punch formula – 1 sweet, 2 sour, 3 strong, 4 weak – but that the "weak" component, generally a juice or a soda, has been swapped for Champagne!

30ml (1fl oz) Vodka - Belvedere
15ml (½fl oz) Crème De Cassis - Merlet Crème De Cassis
25ml (⅘fl oz) Fresh Lemon Juice
10ml (⅓fl oz) Sugar Syrup
Top Champagne - Möet & Chandon Brut

Glassware: Highball
Ice: Block Ice
Garnish: Lemon Slice
Preparation: Quick Shake, Top Champagne

○

Add all the ingredients, except the Champagne, to a shaker with ice and shake.

Strain into a highball glass over ice and top up with Champagne. Stir gently to mix, garnish with a lemon slice and serve.

RUSTY NAIL

This very simple scotch-based digestif is forever associated with the Rat Pack as the classic pairing of Drambuie and scotch was their drink of choice in the 1950s at the 21 Club in New York, and almost defines their laid-back sophistication and cool.

If you enjoy this, try the B & B – it's equal parts cognac and BÉNÉDICTINE D.O.M Liqueur, and made and garnished in the same way.

40ml (1⅓fl oz) Scotch – Johnnie Walker Black Label
20ml (¾fl oz) Drambuie

Glassware: Rocks Glass
Ice: Block Ice
Garnish: Lemon Twist
Preparation: Build

o

Add both ingredients to a rocks glass and stir quickly to mix.
Add ice, garnish with a lemon twist and serve.

SAZERAC

This beautiful cocktail was born in the 1850s in New Orleans. It was born a cognac cocktail and it is named after the brand that it was originally created with – Sazerac de Forge et Fils. The rye version is just as delicious though. The absinthe rinsed glass lets you enjoy the delicate and nuanced aroma.

We also think that it benefits from being poured into a glass from a height as this aerates the drink and gives it a slightly different mouthfeel to that of a Manhattan or Old Fashioned.

If you like this, you can play with it a little and make with both rye and cognac (25ml of both) for what's called a "Half and Half".

Absinthe - Pernod Absinthe
50ml (1¾fl oz) Cognac or Rye - Sazerac Straight Rye or Hennessy V.S.O.P
7.5ml (¼fl oz) Sugar Syrup
2.5ml (4 dashes) Peychaud's Bitters

Glassware: Absinthe-rinsed Rocks Glass
Ice: Served Without
Garnish: Discarded Lemon Twist
Preparation: Long Stir

o

First rinse the chilled rocks glass with absinthe, ensuring the glass is thoroughly coated, and then pour off the excess.

Add all the ingredients to a mixing glass with ice and stir.

Strain into the rocks glass, gently squeeze a lemon twist over the top and then serve.

CHARLES SCHUMANN

—

CAFÉ PEP

1 Brown Sugar Cube
60ml (2fl oz) Brandy Carlos I Solera Grand Reserva
25ml ($^4/_5$fl oz) Cold Espresso
Absinthe Spray

Glassware: Rocks Glass
Ice: Served Without
Garnish: Served Without
Preparation: Build

○

Place the sugar cube in a rocks glass and pour the brandy on top.
Stir until the sugar has dissolved.

Add the espresso and stir, then spray with absinthe and serve.

SHERRY COBBLER

This was an invention of the 1830s and was apparently one of the most popular drinks of the day. It's not hard to see why as it makes a wonderful summer sipper and you can play around with different fruits to suit the seasons. We like swapping out the strawberry and orange for raisins and apple in the autumn.

60ml (2fl oz) Oloroso Sherry - Gonzalez Byass
1 Strawberry
2 Wedges of Orange
1 Slice of Lemon
5ml (⅙fl oz) Sugar Syrup

Glassware: Rocks Glass
Ice: Crushed
Garnish: Mint Sprig
Preparation: Quick Shake

○

Add all the ingredients to a shaker with ice and shake.

Strain into a rocks glass filled with crushed ice, garnish with a sprig of mint and serve.

SIDECAR

This simple sour classic is a taste of London in the 1920s and is believed to have been invented by an Pat McGarry at The Buck's Club.

This recipe may seem a little tart in comparison to many others in the book. However, the sugar rim brings a delicious sweetness, along with a nice textural element.

40ml (1⅓fl oz) Cognac – Remy Martin V.S.O.P
20ml (¾fl oz) Fresh Lemon Juice
20ml (¾fl oz) Orange Curaçao – Pierre Ferrand Dry Curaçao
2.5ml (4 dashes) Sugar Syrup

Glassware: Coupette
Ice: Served Without
Garnish: Sugar Rim
Preparation: Long Shake

o

Prepare a chilled coupette with a sugar rim (see page 31).

Add all the ingredients to a shaker with ice and shake.

Strain into the chilled, sugar-rimmed glass and serve.

SULLIVAN DOH

—

CAR'S DELIGHT

45ml (1½fl oz) Cognac D'USSÉ VSOP
30ml (1fl oz) Pierre Ferrand Dry Curaçao
20ml (¾fl oz) Fresh Lemon Juice
10ml (⅓fl oz) Orange Blossom Water

Glassware: Coupette
Ice: Served Without
Garnish: Served Without
Preparation: Long Shake

○

Add all the ingredients to a shaker with ice and shake.
Strain into a chilled coupette and serve.

SINGAPORE SLING

This long, fruity gin-based cocktail was invented at the beginning of the 20th century by a Hainanese barman called Ngiam Tong Boon, who was working at the Long Bar at Raffles Hotel in Singapore.

There are many different variations of the Singapore Sling in circulation, but this one is our favourite. It's fruity, refreshing and complex due to the myriad of ingredients.

40ml (1⅓fl oz) Gin – Portobello Road Gin
10ml (⅓fl oz) Cherry Brandy – Cherry Heering
5ml (⅙fl oz) BÉNÉDICTINE D.O.M. Liqueur
10ml (⅓fl oz) Grenadine
5ml (⅙fl oz) Triple Sec – Cointreau
1.25ml (2 dashes) Angostura Bitters
25ml (⅘fl oz) Fresh Lemon Juice
Top Soda – Schweppes Soda

Glassware: Highball
Ice: Block Ice
Garnish: Lemon Slice and Maraschino Cherry
Preparation: Short Shake, Top Soda

o

Add all the ingredients, except the soda, to a shaker with ice and shake.

Strain into a highball glass over ice. Top with soda, garnish with a lemon slice and maraschino cherry and serve.

(WHISKEY) SMASH

This is like a minty Whisky Sour (see page 212) or a Mint Julep (see page 145) and although this version was created at the end of the Nineties by Dale DeGroff at The Rainbow Room in New York, the drink has links back to Jerry Thomas's *The Bar-Tender's Guide* of 1887.

It tastes delicious as mint and bourbon are such natural bedfellows and actually works well with almost any spirit base: gin, vodka, rum, tequila... And then if you throw in a few slices of cucumber and switch the lemon to lime, you are into the Maid family of cocktails!

50ml (1¾fl oz) Bourbon - Maker's Mark Bourbon
25ml (⅘fl oz) Fresh Lemon Juice
15ml (½fl oz) Sugar Syrup
6–8 Mint Leaves

Glassware: Rocks Glass
Ice: Block Ice
Garnish: Mint Sprig
Preparation: Medium Shake

o

Add all the ingredients to a shaker with ice and shake.

Strain into a rocks glass over ice and garnish with a sprig of mint.

JAD BALLOUT

—

EL MEDITERRANEO

50ml (1¾fl oz) Bacardi Carta Blanca
20ml (¾fl oz) Fresh Lemon Juice
20ml (¾fl oz) Sugar Syrup 1:1 (see below)
10ml (⅓fl oz) Skinos Mastiha Liqueur
3 Basil Leaves

Glassware: Martini Glass
Ice: Served Without
Garnish: 4 Drops Olive Oil
Preparation: Long Shake

Add all the ingredients to a shaker with ice and shake.
Strain into a chilled martini glass, garnish and serve.

SUGAR SYRUP 1:1

1 Part Caster Sugar
1 Part Water

Stir together and until the sugar is dissolved.

SOUTHSIDE
(OR SOUTH SIDE)

This one goes back to the Prohibition, as a long version of the drink, served over crushed ice, was apparently the drink of the Chicago Southside mobsters. This shorter version, a perfect balance of gin, mint and lime, was created at the 21 Club in New York. Top with Champagne for a Southside Royale, or soda for a Southside Fizz.

50ml (1¾fl oz) Gin - Cotswolds Dry Gin
25ml (⅘fl oz) Fresh Lime Juice
15ml (½fl oz) Sugar Syrup
6–8 Mint Leaves

Glassware: Coupette
Ice: Served Without
Garnish: Mint Leaf
Preparation: Long Shake

o

Add all the ingredients to a shaker with ice and shake.
Strain into a chilled coupette, garnish with a mint leaf and serve.

STINGER

This pre-Prohibition cocktail was created by Reginald Vanderbilt, who was not a bartender but a wealthy businessman who made his money on horses. It is sometimes served over crushed ice but, in our opinion, it more than holds it own straight up. However, make sure you use crème de menthe blanc, instead of its verte counterpart, as otherwise you'll end up with a less appealing colour.

50ml (1¾fl oz) Cognac – Hine Rare V.S.O.P
10ml (⅓fl oz) Crème de Menthe Blanc – Briottet Crème De Menthe Blanc

Glassware: Coupette
Ice: Served Without
Garnish: Mint Leaf
Preparation: Long Stir

○

Add both ingredients to a mixing glass with ice and stir.
Pour into a chilled coupette, garnish with a mint leaf and serve.

TOM COLLINS

The invention of this one is attributed to John Collins, from the Limmer's Hotel in London, towards the end of the 19th century. Essentially, it's almost identical to the Gin Fizz (see page 114), but the difference is that it's served over ice and in a highball. Some recipes call for an Old Tom Gin, hence the name, but in our opinion, a London Dry works just as well. If using an Old Tom, the recipe may need less sugar, so have a taste and see.

1 Lemon Peel to Shake
15ml Chef Spoon (½fl oz) Caster Sugar
30ml (1fl oz) Fresh Lemon Juice
60ml (2fl oz) Gin – No. 3 London Dry Gin
Top Soda – Schweppes Soda

Glassware: Highball
Ice: Block Ice
Garnish: Lemon Slice and Discarded Lemon Coin
Preparation: Quick Shake and Top Soda

○

Add the lemon peel and sugar to a shaker and muddle. Add the lemon juice and stir until the sugar is dissolved. Add the gin with ice and shake.

Strain into a highball glass over ice. Top up with soda water and gently mix. Garnish with a lemon slice, gently squeeze a lemon coin over the top and then serve.

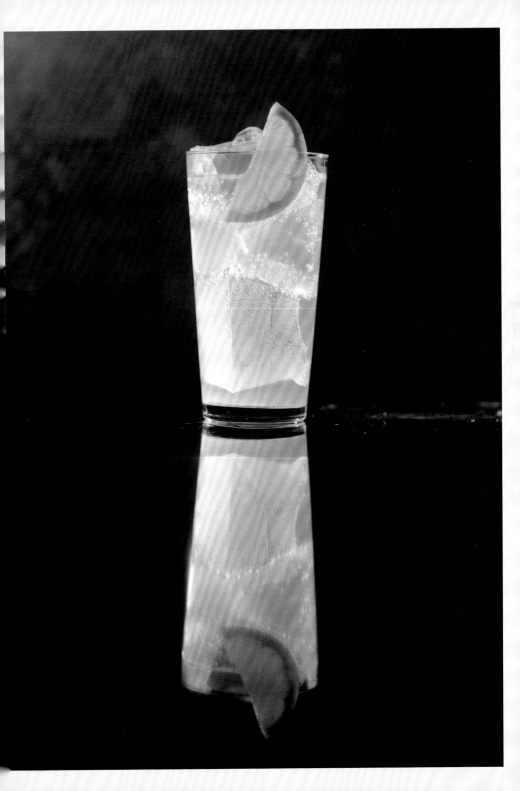

TOMMY'S MARGARITA

This was created in the early nineties by Julio Bermejo in San Francisco at his family restaurant, Tommy's (in ours and many others opinion the premier tequila bar on earth). Julio's knowledge of tequila is legendary and this very simple take on a Margarita is a stroke of genius. Made without the traditional orange liqueur but with agave syrup, it became an instant classic and is now on bar menus worldwide. This recipe was kindly provided by Julio himself.

60ml (2fl oz) Blanco Tequila – L&J Tequila Blanco
30ml (1fl oz) Fresh Persian Lime Juice
30ml (1fl oz) Agave Syrup (1 part agave
syrup mixed with 1 part filtered water)

Glassware: Rocks Glass
Ice: Block Ice
Garnish: Lime Wheel
Preparation: Medium Shake

°

Add all the ingredients to a shaker with ice and shake.
Strain into a chilled rocks glass over ice, garnish with a lime wheel and serve.

TUXEDO

This is a very interesting riff on the Martini (see page 142). It first appeared in print in Harry Johnson's *Bartenders' Manual* of 1900, but had been on the scene for a while before that.

The original recipe calls for equal parts sweet gin (Old Tom) and dry vermouth, with 2 dashes of maraschino, 1 dash of absinthe and 2 or 3 dashes of orange bitters. However, over time there have been many variations on the theme, and by the time it was printed in *The Savoy Cocktail Book* (1930), there was a clear delineation between a Tuxedo No. 1 and a Tuxedo No. 2. The former was equal parts dry gin and dry vermouth with lemon peel and absinthe, and the latter was the same but with maraschino and orange bitters. Therefore, technically, the recipe below is a Tuxedo No. 2. Deliciously complex and aromatic, we recommend you try them both.

30ml (1fl oz) Gin - Fords Gin
30ml (1fl oz) Dry Vermouth - Noilly Prat Original
1.25ml (2 dashes) Orange Bitters - Regans' Orange Bitter No.6
1.25ml (2 dashes) Absinthe - Pernod Absinthe
2.5ml (4 dashes) Maraschino - Luxardo Maraschino

Glassware: Coupette
Ice: Served Without
Garnish: Lemon Coin
Preparation: Long Stir

o

Add all the ingredients to a mixing glass with ice and stir.

Strain into a chilled coupette, garnish with a lemon coin and serve.

MONICA BERG

—

JASMINE

55ml (1⅘fl oz) Hepple Gin
15ml (½fl oz) Noilly Prat Original
15ml (½fl oz) MUYU Jasmine Verte

Glassware: Coupette
Ice: Served Without
Garnish: Kalamata Olive
Preparation: Long Stir

o

Add all the ingredients to a mixing glass with ice and stir.
Pour into a chilled coupette, garnish with a kalamata olive and serve.

VESPER

The Vesper first appeared in print in 1953 and not in a cocktail book, but in Ian Fleming's first James Bond novel *Casino Royale* and was inspired by the author's numerous trips to Dukes Hotel in London. It's a type of Martini that is always shaken, never stirred, which aerates the drink and serves it up colder and a little more diluted than other Martinis. It used to be made with Kina Lillet (a French quinine-flavoured aromatised wine), a now-discontinued product, but Cocchi Americano (an Italian herb- and spice-infused product) brings to the drink a subtle bitterness, which helps give the cocktail depth.

45ml (1½fl oz) Gin – Star of Bombay Gin
15ml (½fl oz) Vodka – Grey Goose
7.5ml (¼fl oz) Cocchi Americano

Glassware: Martini Glass
Ice: Served Without
Garnish: Lemon Coin
Preparation: Long Shake

o

Add all the ingredients to a shaker with ice and shake.

Strain into a chilled martini glass, garnish with a lemon coin and serve.

VIEUX CARRÉ

This is another New Orleans classic (1938) that comes from Walter Bergeron at the Carousel Bar at the Monteleone Hotel and is named after the French term for the city's famed French Quarter.

It's a stunning digestif and something that all Old Fashioned and Sazerac (see page 158 and 189) fans should try at some point. In our opinion, it's certainly not made often enough.

25ml (⅘fl oz) Rye – Michter's US*1 Straight Rye
25ml (⅘fl oz) Cognac – Remy Martin V.S.O.P
25ml (⅘fl oz) Sweet Vermouth – Asterley Bros. Estate English Vermouth
5ml (⅙fl oz) BÉNÉDICTINE D.O.M. Liqueur
1.25ml (2 dashes) Angostura Bitters
1.25ml (2 dashes) Peychaud's Bitters

Glassware: Rocks Glass
Ice: Block Ice
Garnish: Lemon Twist
Preparation: Medium Stir

o

Add all the ingredients to a mixing glass with ice and stir.
Strain into an ice-filled rocks glass, garnish with a lemon twist and serve.

RYAN CLIFT

—

TRUFFLE SHUFFLE

50ml (1¾fl oz) Hennessey V.S.O.P
5ml (⅙fl oz) Sugar Syrup
45ml (1½fl oz) Truffle Shuffle Mix (see below)

Glassware: Rocks Glass
Ice: Block Ice
Garnish: Sprig of Thyme, Black Truffle Slice and Discarded Orange coin
Preparation: Stir

○

Add all the ingredients to a mixing glass with ice and stir.
Pour into a rocks glass over ice and garnish.

TRUFFLE SHUFFLE MIX

10ml Madeira
20ml Ruby Port
2 Bar Spoons (10ml or ⅓fl oz) Truffle Juice
1 Bar Spoon (5ml or ⅙fl oz) Thyme Tips

Infuse all these ingredients together for 8 hours and then strain.

WHISKY SOUR

This classic belongs to the Sour family of cocktails and is a simple and delicious drink. Created in the 1850s, it wasn't until almost 50 years later that egg white became an extra addition. Some recipes list it as optional, but we like to include it as we think it helps round out the flavours.

You can also switch out the bourbon for scotch, applejack, cognac or pretty much any spirit – any type that has spent time in a barrel tends to work best.

50ml (1¾fl oz) Bourbon - Woodford Reserve Bourbon
25ml (⅘fl oz) Fresh Lemon Juice
15ml (½fl oz) Sugar Syrup
25ml (⅘fl oz) Egg White

Glassware: Coupette
Ice: Served Without
Garnish: Angostura Bitters Stripe
Preparation: Dry Shake and Long Wet Shake

o

Add all the ingredients to a shaker and dry shake, followed by a wet shake (with ice).

Strain into a chilled coupette, garnish with an Angostura bitters stripe and serve.

WHITE LADY

The White Lady is a lovely light, sour classic and its invention is contested by two famous Harrys in the bar world. The first is Harry MacElhone, who initially created a White Lady with crème de menthe and lemon and orange liqueur at Ciro's Club in London and then swapped the menthe to gin in 1929. However, Harry Craddock is also credited with making the drink when it was added to *The Savoy Cocktail Book* of 1930.

The egg white was a later addition, but we like to preserve it as it rounds off all the beautiful citrus notes in the drink. However, it is important to dry shake first before you add the ice, to achieve the right texture.

40ml (1⅓fl oz) Gin - Ki No Bi Kyoto Dry Gin
10ml (⅓fl oz) Triple Sec - Cointreau
25ml (⅘fl oz) Fresh Lemon Juice
10ml (⅓fl oz) Sugar Syrup
25ml (⅘fl oz) Egg White

Glassware: Coupette
Ice: Served Without
Garnish: Discarded Lemon Coin
Preparation: Dry Shake and Long Wet Shake

o

Add all the ingredients to a shaker and dry shake, followed by a wet shake (with ice).

Strain into a chilled coupette, gently squeeze a lemon coin over the top and then serve.

ERIK LORINCZ

—

GREEN PARK

50ml (1¾fl oz) Jensen's Old Tom Gin
30ml (1fl oz) Fresh Lemon Juice
15ml (½fl oz) Sugar Syrup
25ml (⅘fl oz) Egg White
3 dashes of Celery Bitters
5 Basil Leaves

Glassware: Coupette
Ice: Served Without
Garnish: Served Without
Preparation: Dry Shake and Long Wet Shake

o

Add all the ingredients to a shaker and dry shake,
followed by a wet shake (with ice).
Strain into a chilled coupette and serve.

WHITE NEGRONI

Created in France in 2001 by Wayne Collins, this is a wonderful riff on a classic Negroni. It swaps out the Campari for Suze (a bitter French aperitif), and the vermouth for Lillet Blanc (a sweet French aperitif wine). It's a little lighter in flavour as well as colour, yet still packs a bittersweet punch like its counterpart. The grapefruit twist adds an interesting dimension compared to the classic orange.

25ml (⅘fl oz) Gin – Beefeater 24
25ml (⅘fl oz) Suze
25ml (⅘fl oz) Lillet Blanc

Glassware: Rocks Glass
Ice: Block Ice
Garnish: Lemon Twist
Preparation: Build

○

Add all the ingredients to a rocks glass with ice and stir quickly.
Garnish with a lemon twist and serve.

RICARDO DYNAN

—

ABSOLUT GANGSTER

60ml (2fl oz) Absolut Original
12.5ml (⅖fl oz) Lillet Blanc
5ml (⅙fl oz) Sugar Syrup
4 drops of Bob's Abbotts Bitters

Glassware: Rocks Glass
Ice: Block Ice
Garnish: Orange Twist
Preparation: Medium Stir

o

Add all the ingredients to a mixing glass with ice and stir.

Pour into a rocks glass over ice, garnish with an orange twist and serve.

WHITE RUSSIAN

The exact origins of this drink are unknown, except that it first appeared in print in 1965 in the USA, and is the creamy counterpart to the equally popular Black Russian.

Shaking the vodka and cream together helps you create a White Russian with a smooth texture and also with alcohol all the way through. Otherwise, the vodka and liqueur are often sat at the bottom which means the last few sips are almost overly potent.

30ml (1fl oz) Vodka - Reyka
20ml (¾fl oz) Heavy Cream
20ml (¾fl oz) Coffee Liqueur - Mr. Black Cold Brew Coffee Liqueur

Glassware: Rocks Glass
Ice: Block Ice
Garnish: Served Without
Preparation: Dry Shake and Float

o

Place the vodka and cream in a shaker and dry shake.

Pour into a rocks glass over ice and float over the coffee liqueur. Serve.

ZOMBIE

This one is a heady, fruity mix of four different kinds of rum, created by the Hollywood restaurateur Ernest Raymond Beaumont Gantt, AKA Don the Beachcomber. We favour his recipe from 1950, apparently, it's a failsafe hangover cure. Handle with care...

25ml (⅘fl oz) White Rum - Plantation 3 Stars White Rum
25ml (⅘fl oz) Gold Rum - Banks 7 Golden Rum
25ml (⅘fl oz) 151 Demerara Rum - Gosling's Black Seal 151 Proof
25ml (⅘fl oz) Fresh Lemon Juice
25ml (⅘fl oz) Fresh Lime Juice
25ml (⅘fl oz) Fresh Pineapple Juice
15ml (½fl oz) Passion Fruit Syrup
15ml (½fl oz) Brown Sugar Syrup
1 dash of Angostura Bitters

Glassware: Hurricane
Ice: Crushed Ice
Garnish: Mint Sprig
Preparation: Quick Shake

o

Add all the ingredients to a shaker with ice and shake.
Strain into a hurricane glass filled with crushed ice.
Garnish with a sprig of mint and serve.

LYNDON HIGGINSON

—

THE CAPTAIN LYNDON ZOMBIE

70ml (2½fl oz) Zombie Mix (see below)
50ml (1¾fl oz) Fresh Orange Juice
50ml (1¾fl oz) Fresh Pineapple Juice
50ml (1¾fl oz) Fresh Apple Juice
50ml (1¾fl oz) Fresh Guava Juice
25ml (⅘fl oz) Fresh Lime Juice

Glassware: Tankard
Ice: Dirty Ice and Crushed Ice Cap
Garnish: Spent Lime Shell, Sugar Cube Soaked in 151, Ground Cinnamon
Preparation: Quick Shake

o

Add all the ingredients to a shaker with ice and shake. Strain into a chilled tankard. Carefully set fire to the sugar cube and dust over the cinnamon.

ZOMBIE MIX

70ml (2½fl oz) Appleton Rum
70ml (2½fl oz) Havana Especial
70ml (2½fl oz) Havana 3
35ml (1¼fl oz) Duppy Share Rum
35ml (1¼fl oz) Caña Brava

35ml (1¼fl oz) Falernum
35ml (1¼fl oz) Cherry Brandy
25ml (⅘fl oz) Vanilla Syrup
12.5ml (⅖fl oz) Passion Fruit Syrup
10ml (⅓fl oz) Absinthe

INDEX

ACKNOWLEDGEMENTS

Our Family
For always supporting us

Our colleagues
For teaching us

Our Publisher
For being so patient

Our Optician
Martin Wolstencroft

Our favourite brothers from Manchester
The Vennings

Our friends Liam Cotter and Matthew
Robertson at Heads, Hearts and Tails
The wind beneath our wings

Our glassware supplier
Artis

Our photographer
Ed Schofield, no relation.